TABLE of CONTENTS

· · · · · ·

. . . .

INTRODUCTION

. . . .

As I begin writing the introduction for this book, I am about to enter my twenty-sixth year of pastoral ministry. To say that things have changed in the church would be a major understatement. Pastor David Jeremiah wrote a book a few years ago titled *I Never Thought I'd See the Day*. He wrote, "When I look at the changes that have occurred in the land I love—and in the church I love even more—just in my lifetime, I have to pinch myself to see if it's a dream" (cited from book jacket cover).

Truly it is not a dream—the church is not what she used to be. But there is strong hope. God is still firmly planted on the throne, and we still have His Word.

In the past twenty-five years I have watched as much of the church world has emphasized a light gospel in salvation and an even lighter gospel in the sanctifying process of making disciples. False teaching has infiltrated the church and has become institutional in many denominations and even more so in congregations that boast of a new way of doing church.

However, the biggest problem could be in the modern church's forgetfulness in how to both fight against false teaching and foster true teaching in our churches. For the last year, First Baptist Church of Jackson, Georgia, the church I have the joy of pastoring, has been walking the path of apprenticeship at the feet of Jesus. Our church has been transformed by the living Word of God.

Now it is time for us to dive in to answer a question that was asked by a member a few weeks ago: "What's next?" Oh, the joy that came to my heart as I heard this question! The way back for the American church is to come back to the feet of Jesus (Revelation 2:1–5). When firmly restored to God, the church must ask, "What's next?"

Brothers and sisters, the answer is before us. God has written His Word as our road map from start to finish in the Christian journey of faith (Philippians 1:6). *His Word* is what is next!

The book you hold in your hands is simply a devotion book based on the truth of God's Word. I have chosen John's writings identified as 1 John as my guide for our "what's next." This devotional book promises help in discovering how to walk in the "what's next" of our faith.

I want to invite you to join me for this journey as we discover how to push back the darkness of false teaching. Join me as we discover how to foster love, scale the heights of who God is, walk in obedience, deal with sin, and overcome the darkness of this world. By the time we are finished you may be able to say, "God has brought me to a place of maturity."

The outline of this book is very similar to that of my first devotion book. You will be given twenty-one devotions. Eighteen come from 1 John and the other three come from 2 and 3 John. Always read the focal text first and the devotion second. Once you have completed the focal text and the devotion, you will be asked to spend the next five days reading selected books of the Bible. Each day's reading has two questions for you to answer. By the end of the week you will have greater understanding of how to live out God's Word.

I pray God's greatest blessing on your life as you seek to grow in the grace and knowledge of who He is. Always remember: we are in this together.

Keith
John 3:30

* * * * * * * *

WHAT'S NEXT?

THE CONFESSIONS OF
AN APPRENTICE

KEITH JOSEPH

dustjacket

🞄dustjacket
www.dustjacket.com

WEEK ONE

The Testimony of One Who Knew
1 John 1:1–4

O ne of the craziest things about people is this: Everyone has an opinion. I want you to think this through with me. Regardless of the subject one would name, everyone will have some opinion.

I have literally been in meetings where someone had no clue of the subject but nevertheless gave his or her opinion of what should happen. A true funny story comes to mind. Years ago I was in a deacons' meeting discussing with the guys about ceasing having monthly business meetings in favor of having them quarterly. One of our older deacons who was a very simple but Spirit-filled man offered his genuine opinion. He said, and I quote: "Pastor, I really have no experience with quarterly business meetings, so I have no opinion. But I did grow up in a church that held their business meetings every three months, and they seemed to work well." Are you smiling yet?

Yes, it is true some questions have more importance than others. For example, is Jesus God's Son? Did Jesus become a man? Did Jesus really die? These questions culminate with one major question: Is Jesus the Savior I need?

The first four verses of I John are John's answer to such questions. As you pick up your Bible to read these verses, it seems as if John is engaged in a discussion with people who had different opinions. The truth is—this is exactly what John is doing.

The Westminster Confession of Faith offers us a summary of what the church believed and believes concerning Jesus:

> God chose and ordained Jesus, His eternal Son, to be the head and Savior of His people. Jesus, the second person of the Trinity, of one substance and equal to the Father, retained His deity while taking on the nature of a man, being born of the virgin Mary, and is therefore fully God, fully man, and fully equipped as the only mediator between God and man. As such, Jesus fulfilled the law, suffered in body and soul, was crucified, died, buried, and resurrected, as-

cended to heaven, intercedes for believers, and will return in judgment. The perfect obedience and sacrificial death of Jesus fully satisfied God's justice, securing redemption for all the elect. The benefits of which are applied by the Holy Spirit to all true believers, even those who lived before Christ's incarnation (Summary of Westminster Confession, by Roy Bennett).

John is seeking to inform his readers about the one person who has changed his life. This one person charted a new course for his life. Now thirty years later, his passion for Jesus has not ceased but is more consuming than ever. John offers us two titles for Jesus in these verses:

- Jesus is the one who is from the beginning. He is the eternal God.

John is filled with wonder and awe of this God. He thinks back to those three-plus years of hearing the voice of God speaking daily. He seems to rise to great joy in remembering the life and ministry of Jesus. I wonder what scenes must have been in John's mind as the Holy Spirit guided him through the first verses of this book. Could it have been when Jesus raised the widow's son in the city of Nain in Luke 7:11–17? Daily John gazed upon the wonder and majesty of this God.

John is decisive in letting us know that Jesus is real. He touched Him and saw Jesus day in and day out. John was there when Jesus died. John saw where they laid Him. John saw the empty tomb, and John saw the resurrected Jesus.

This is the testimony of one who believed.

• Jesus is the Word of life.

John has good news for his readers: this life was revealed (manifested). John is writing to testify of this truth. He wants his readers to know that the Son of God was existing with the Father for all time. The Son of God came to the earth to purchase our redemption.

John wants his readers to know Jesus so that they also can have the joy he possessed and so they can be in the family of God. He knew his joy would overflow as people made Jesus the Lord of their lives.

This week I want to challenge you with Scriptures that will help you answer the question "Who is Jesus?"

Day 1:

Read Luke 1

and answer the following questions:

• Why was it important for Jesus to be born of a virgin? Consider Galatians 4:3–4 in your answer.

• Would a person go to hell if he or she lived a life free from sin from birth?

Day 2:

Read Luke 23

and answer the following questions:

- Did Jesus have a real human body? How do you know one way or the other?
- Was Jesus' body like ours before the crucifixion? What type of body does He have in heaven?

Day 3:

Read Hebrews 5

and answer the following questions:

- How did Jesus live His life on the earth?
- How does His example challenge you to live your life?

Day 4:

Read Hebrews 9

and answer the following questions:

- Why is it so important for Jesus to be sinless?
- If Jesus was sinless, then why did He learn obedience, according to Hebrews 5?

Day 5:

Read Hebrews 4

and answer the following questions:

- Was it possible for Jesus to sin? Could Jesus have sinned?
- Is it possible for you to live a life apart from sin?

WEEK TWO

The Answer for Our Darkness
1 John 1:5–10

A s I sit down before my computer, our nation is grieving the death of seventeen students who were viciously gunned down at Marjory Stoneman Douglas High School in Parkland, Florida, on February 14, 2018. People in all walks of life are pointing fingers as to who is at fault. A groundswell of people believe the fault lies with the easy access Americans have to weapons of mass destruction.

Steven Kerr, coach of the NBA Golden State Warriors, blamed the government when he said, "How crazy to focus on building a wall when the real issue is the lack of gun control" (interview with ESPN, "Sports Center," February 16, 2018).

One can understand Steve's anger, having lost his father to a vicious murder in 1984. But is the answer to our world's darkness simply taking away assault rifles? Still others suggest the problem lies with the inequality between the rich and poor. Could it be that most people are totally overlooking the true reason for our darkness as a nation? Is it possible that the darkness that engulfs our world needs a solution that is beyond our ability to solve?

When we look back to the days of Jesus, we are reminded of His timeless answer to the burning question of our day:

> *Again Jesus spoke to them, saying, "I am the light of the world. Whoever follows me will not walk in darkness, but will have the light of life" (John 8:12).*

Jesus taught us of the true source of darkness, our own sinfulness, which stands in opposition to God and His direction of our lives. Jesus clearly deals with this same truth in John 3:16–21.

In this week's focal text, John draws a circle around the real issue and shines the light of the gospel on the truth of the only answer for our darkness. Our world will continue to reside in and be ruled by the darkness until she embraces the light of Jesus. This is the answer for our darkness.

Walk with John through John 1:5–10 as you seek to understand how the answer can be yours as well as that of your fellow man. The answer for our darkness requires three steps on our part in coming to the light:

- Simply be honest.

Jesus is not the source of our darkness. He has no sin in His life. There will never be a moment when we will unearth dirt on Jesus. But the truth is, you cannot say this about my life. Nor can you say it about your life. The truth is, I was born in the darkness. I lived as a child in the darkness. In my life I have never met anyone who had a different story that this.

Have you come to this place of honesty? Have you come to understand that the darkness in this world is your fault and my fault? We are each spiritually burnt-out light bulbs seeking to bring light to the darkness in the world. The light is not in us—it is in Jesus. I truly am not the answer to the world's problems. I have my own problems. In honesty, we need help from an outside source.

- Take the step of humility.

It is very hard for sinners to own the darkness because they are living in a dark world. If we keep holding onto the belief that we are not the problem, we will live in even deeper darkness. Even the apostles had to admit that they were redeemed sinners (1 Timothy 1:15–16).

Take time this week to look at your life under the microscope of God's light. Do you and I need a fresh touch of humility that cries out to God, "I am a sinner who needs a Savior"?

- Step into happiness.

When a person accepts what John has written, the person admits his or her sin and asks God to forgive his or her sin. Happiness comes as the person receive the forgiveness of God. In this moment the darkness rolls away. In this moment the light of Jesus fills the mind of the believer, who now will experience the happiness of living a life in the light seeking to push back the darkness of this world.

I want to challenge you to a deeper understanding of the difference between the darkness and light. Take the time to genuinely allow the Scripture to shine on every part of your character as well as your theology of life.

Assignments for the week:

Day 1:

Read John 3

and answer the following questions:

- Why was Nicodemus coming to Jesus at night? Is there a reason that people do so many evil deeds under the cover of darkness?

- Do you ever struggle with living in a dark world? Give specific examples.

Day 2:

Read John 7–8

and answer the following questions:

- What was the significance of Jesus' proclamation in John 7: 37–38? Describe how the "Water of life" and the "Light of the world" can change the world.
- What difference has the Water and Light made in your life? Give specific examples.

Day 3:

Read John 12

and answer the following questions:

- Why was the Light with the people for just a short time?
- Why does the darkness overcome people, nations, and sometimes even Christians? Be specific in your answers.

Day 4:

Read John 15

and answer the following questions:

- Is it possible to live with unconfessed sins while

having close fellowship with Jesus? Think about your thought life and your life of service in your answer.

- Who are your closest friends? Do you find their friendship and your friendship centered around Christ?

Day 5:

Read John 19–20

and answer the following questions:

- Why did Jesus have to go to the cross?
- What impact does the blood of Jesus have upon your interpretation of 1 John 1:9? Explain how God has dealt with your personal sins.

* * * * * * * *

WEEK THREE

What Did I Do?
John 2:1–6

here I was sitting in front of my computer screen with the look of disgust. I found myself so upset because I could not find the file that I was looking for. I knew I had completed the manuscript for the message I was about to take with me to a pastor's conference. But it was not to be found.

In transparency I began to wonder if I had even written the sermon. Was I losing it at this early age or was there a devouring file monster in my laptop? I looked under every file and was about to give up, but by the grace of God I suddenly found the file under another title.

Oh, how frustrating life can be when you know you have lost something that is valuable to you!

In this week's focal passage, John is continuing to instruct the believer about his or her new life in Christ. The subject matter is about this issue of losing something. The something is our salvation.

I cannot wait until the question section of our study. I have to ask you now: Can someone lose his or her salvation? The question comes as a result of John's writing before us.

John begins chapter two with these simple words: "My little children." The Greek text could be translated "little born-again ones." Who are these people? They are the people who in chapter one were honest about their sin nature—they humbled themselves and repented of their sin; they were made happy by the forgiveness of sins they received in and through Christ alone. They were what Christians call "saved." They are "little born-again ones."

This is so important. John's letter is to them. Here is how I interpret the first part of verse one: I am writing under the inspiration of the Holy Spirit so that you can sin less and less. I do not want you to sin, but you will.

Brothers and sisters, there will be moments when you will fail God. You will miss the mark (perhaps even sin). As I write this devotion, my heart is heavy because I had one of those moments just this morning.

When believers sin there are questions that come:

- Am I still saved?
- Did I lose my salvation?
- Was I really ever saved?
- Do I need to be saved again?

These are genuine questions that need a true answer from God! Brethren we have our answer before us in our focal text. John says that when you sin, and you will sin, there are things put in place in your life that assure you that you are still saved.

You have an advocate in your life.

The word *advocate* is the Greek word *parkakletos,* which means one who helps and one who comes alongside us.

When a believer sins, the fellowship between the believer and God is broken. When the sinner repents of his or her sin to God (1:9), Jesus becomes his or her defense attorney before God. John MacArthur says, "Jesus accepts as clients only those who confess their guilt and their desperate need to receive Him as Savior and Lord" (*MacArthur New Testament Commentary, 1–3 John,* 47).

Jesus comes before the judgment bar of God (the mercy seat). We come with Him. Jesus speaks to the Father on our behalf. He defends us in a very unusual way. He says, "He pleads guilty. But I am here to pay his debt. I am his propitiation." He is our what? Jesus offers a payment to God for our sin. This is amazing, brothers and sisters! Jesus took the wrath that was due to me. I am even more amazed when I realize that God the Father accepts His payment in my place. In the moment this happens, fellowship is restored between me and God. I am still saved.

You have an altar with God.

Never forget that God gives you access through Jesus into His very throne room (Hebrews 4:14–16; 9:9–16). Daily I come before the altar of God in the morning when I get up, throughout the day, and finally when I lie down at night. My advocate is always on the job.

You have a new attitude from God.

Your life is now different. You do not desire to sin. Rebellion is the last thing on your mind. You are broken when you sin. This new attitude is an assurance that you have not lost your salvation nor will you ever lose it because it has been given to you by God.

John warns us about having no remorse for our sin. If you live your life without an altar and without an attitude change, it is proof positive that you do not have an advocate with the Father. But you *can* have Jesus as your advocate. At the back of this book is a step-by-step guide that will help you make this most important decision.

As a "little born-again one," take time to settle the issue of losing one's salvation in this week's assignments.

Assignments for the week:

Day 1:
Read Ephesians 1–2
and answer the following questions:

- What did God have to do so man could be saved?
- What does a person have to do in order to be saved?

Day 2:

Read Ephesians 3

and answer the following questions:

- What did Paul mean by "the unfathomable riches of Christ" (NASB)?
- As you read Paul's prayer in this chapter, write down how God has answered those prayers in your life.

Day 3:

Read Ephesians 4

and answer the following questions:

- How important is it to know how to walk with God?
- What role does the church play in keeping fellow believers on the correct path?

Day 4:

Read Ephesians 5

and answer the following questions:

- What changes have you experienced in your life since Jesus has become your advocate?

- What role does the Holy Spirit play in the protecting and perfecting of your faith?

Day 5:

Read Ephesians 6

and answer the following questions:

- How does the truth of our focal text help us to be "strong in the Lord"?
- Which part of the armor of God seems the hardest for you to put on daily?

* * * * * * * *

WEEK FOUR

Love Verses Hate
1 John 2:7–11

* * * * * * * *

It was a day when the small family of four would face a moment that would forever change the course of their lives. If there had been one, the police report would have read, "Older brother murders younger brother." A closer look identifies the truth of there being much more to this tragic moment.

Both the father and mother had responsibility in what happened. It was they who passed onto the boys a sinful nature. But certainly this does not in any way excuse the vicious sin of the older brother. Each brother was responsible for his own choices. One brother obeyed what God asked and the other decided to disobey what God asked. The older brother became envious of his younger brother. His envy led to bitterness, which in turn led to anger that blew out of control on this tragic day. He rose up and killed his brother. It was plain and simple murder.

Darkness engulfed the family on this dreaded day. Their world would never be the same. Such was the story of Cain and Abel. You can read their entire story in Genesis 4.

Since that day there have been countless murders in our world. The word *murder* in its simplest definition is defined as "the unlawful premeditated killing of one human being by another." Murder takes on many forms in our society. Here is a short list: the taking of innocent lives by genocide, euthanasia, abortion; innocents killed in war, hate crimes, drive-by shootings, and being in the wrong place at the wrong time.

As I write this devotion there have been twelve school shootings during the first nine weeks of this year. Each year the number of mass shootings continues to rise. The question comes: *What does God have to say about this?* And an even bigger question is *What does God offer as a solution to this terrible world of hate?*

Our focal text offers us two answers from God:

- John says, "God's answer is in the form of an old command" (v. 7).

Brothers and sisters, what old commandment can help with a new problem? Imagine that an advertising company had as their jingle "Buy our old product—it is better than the new." Ours is a society that is crazed with the view that new and improved is always better than the old and worn. However, this is exactly what John places before us. The old John writes about this:

> You shall not hate your brother in your heart, but you shall reason frankly with your neighbor, lest you incur sin because of him. You shall not take vengeance or bear a grudge against the sons of your own people, but you shall love your neighbor as yourself: I am the LORD (Leviticus 19:17–19).

When God's people were established at Mount Sinai, God gave them the Ten Commandments. One of the ten was this: "Do not murder" (Exodus 20:13). God values all human beings. He proved this by going to the cross (John 3:16). In a world filled with hate, God taught us to love one another. This is an old commandment.

- John says, "God's answer is in the form of a new command" (v. 8).

This new commandment is worded just like the old commandment. The question is *What makes it new?* The answer is so awesome. The old commandment was given to tell us what not to do. But men could not keep from doing what was wrong, because evil dwelled within them. But when Christ came, He modeled a new way. All those who surrender their lives to Him move from the law of "Do not murder" to the liberation of love—"I will not murder."

These two commandments are God's answer to the hate in our world. We need the commandment of Exodus 20 to show us why we are hating people, and we need the commandment of 1 John 4:8, which teaches us of Jesus' words in Matthew 5:43–45 and Matthew 22:37–38 so that we know how to love.

Take time this week to work through each day's assignments with a heart to follow the commandments.

Day 1:

Read Genesis 4

and answer the following questions:

- Why did Cain boil over in anger toward his brother? Think about what God had required of him.
- What issues of anger are at work in our society today? Where do you find yourself in the debates?

Day 2:

Read Leviticus 19

and answer the following questions:

- Why did God have to be so specific in his moral laws with His chosen people?
- Why do people often attempt to make allowances for sin because of their unique circumstances? List a few of the common ones in our day.

Day 3:

Read Romans 12–14

and answer the following questions:

- What has to happen to one's mind-set before he or she can follow the command of God? Interact with Romans 12 in your answer.
- What impact does Jesus' teaching have on your daily walk? Consider Romans 13:9–14 in your answer.

Day 4:

Read John 13

and answer the following questions:

- Did Peter love Jesus as much as Jesus loved Peter? Think through the event of the foot washing.
- What will have to transpire in our nation before people will start loving each other?

Day 5:

Read Proverbs 4–6

and answer the following questions:

- What warnings did the writer offer to those who wanted to follow God?
- What are the common things Christians do to cause others to stumble? Be honest about your own life in your answer.

⁕ ⁕ ⁕ ⁕ ⁕ ⁕ ⁕ ⁕

WEEK FIVE

The Next Level
1 John 2:12–14

From my earliest days as a pastor, I have always had this theory stuck in my mind. The theory has been one of the many drivers in my life that have led me to strive to keep growing in my walk with Christ. It has been with me in good times, bad times, great times, and not-so-good times. This theory is simply as follows:

- God has different levels of growth in one's Christian life.

We see this ideal of growth throughout the Bible. There are over thirty uses of the word *growth* in the New Testament. One of those is in 2 Thessalonians 1:3—"We ought always to give thanks to God for you, brothers, as is right, because your faith is growing abundantly, and the love of every one of you for one another is increasing."

We hear the apostle Peter as he cries out from the past: "Grow" (2 Peter 3:18).

God intends for His children to grow from level one to level three in their walk with Him. Now this may be the first time you are hearing about these levels. If so, or if this is your one-hundredth time, I want you to read with fresh eyes our focal text. Do not read the rest of the devotion until you have read 1 John 2:12–14.

Be assured: all of John's teaching is directed toward two groups of people. He addresses his writing to those who are outside the family of God and to those who are in the family of God. To the outsiders he writes, "The gospel leads you to salvation." To the insiders he writes, "Growth leads to sanctification."

John specifically points out our need for growth of our faith. Before us are the three levels of growth in our Christian lives: those of "little children," "young men," and "spiritual fathers."

We must understand that these are not separate groups being identified here. There is one group, the insiders, who have different levels of spiritual growth. Be assured that God wants you to grow in your spiritual life. MacArthur writes, "When growth is hindered in the physical realm either by malnutrition, disease, or birth defects, the results can be tragic. But it is an even greater tragedy when believers fail to grow and mature spiritually" (*MacArthur New Testament Commentary, 1–3 John,* 69).

Ask yourself, "At what level am I in my walk with God?" Below you will read about the three levels.

Level 1: God brings you into His family.

This is a total work of grace (1 John 1:7; 2:1–2). The blood of Jesus does the cleansing for us (Acts 10:43). Christ-followers have an assurance they have been forgiven. This first level is never reached by the masses of people. This level gives you access to the Father in prayer, petition, and praise. Those who go to this level have a long journey ahead, but it is a joyous journey with Jesus.

Level 2: God strengthens you in daily life.

The Lord gives believers the Holy Spirit to ensure their growth possibilities (1 John 4:4). The person who wants to grow now has a deeper hunger for the Word of God and for the service of God. The Word of God becomes the believer's guide, and the Spirit of God is his or her conviction. These days of growth are not without trial. But daily the believer will endure the trials of life while looking forward to what is ahead.

Level 3: God establishes you in the family.

John identifies this level as the level for "fathers." The believer has come to intimacy with the Heavenly Father. Such a believer knows he or she has been saved for such a time as this. The intimacy is amazing at this level. The Father has mentored such a believer with the goal of directing him or her to mentor other people. Such a person's influence will be felt far and wide because of his or her growth in Christ.

Ask yourself again, "At what level am I in my walk with Christ?"

In your readings this week you will be able to discover the depths of your answer. If by grace you discover that you are at Level 3, be assured that you are not through yet. Read the words of Paul: "Excel still more" (1 Thessalonians 4:10, NASB).

Take time this week to work through each day's assignments with a desire to get to the next level:

Day 1:

Read Acts 16

and answer the following questions:

- Who were the first three church members in the Philippian church? How must they have gotten along together?
- Did each of them have a different way he or she came to salvation? Explain.

Day 2:

Read Philippians 1

and answer the following questions:

- According to verse 6, how is God involved in every level of one's spiritual growth?
- In what ways can believers walk worthy of the gospel?

Day 3:

Read Philippians 2

and answer the following questions:

- What was on Christ's mind as He walked on the earth?
- How does one work out his or her salvation?

Day 4:

Read Philippians 3

and answer the following questions:

- Why did Paul come to the place of rejecting all his religious efforts to get to the next level of faith? Include in your answer "The fellowship of His death."
- According to Paul, how does one "press forward"?

Day 5:

Read Philippians 4

and answer the following questions:

- The two women who had issues needed help in their growth. What suggestions would you make to these women?
- In what ways can the truth of Philippians 4:13 encourage a believer in each level of growth?

* * * * * * * *

WEEK SIX

Don't Slip
1 John 2:15–17

A nyone who knows me knows that I grew up in the mountains of eastern Kentucky. My early life was filled with laughter, hard work, and much adventure. Every summer I would get to spend time in the mountains, or as flatlanders would say, "the hills."

My teenage summers were spent exploring the mountains on dirt bikes with my friends. Years later I returned to some of those places. I thought, "I wouldn't even walk on those places now!" I realized that if my friends or I had even slightly slipped off one of those trails, there would have been major damage if not loss of our lives.

As John continues to write to the church about their next steps of faith, he suddenly, with bold emphasis, writes, *Do not*. I hope you see the seriousness of what John is writing. The child of God who has progressed in his or her faith to the level of fatherhood (2:12–14) must beware of slipping in his or her faith.

Be assured that John is not referring to losing one's salvation. His Lord and our Lord taught the disciples of the impossibility of this being the case (John 10:27–30; 17:7–20). However, John is referring to something that will cause the child of God to slip in his or her faith.

What is this mysterious thing that could cause a child of God to lose ground in faith? What is this monster that could capture the attention and even the passion of a child of God? What is this master of deceit that would enslave the life of a child of God?

John's answer is at the end of His command: "Do not *love the world*" (1 John 2:15, italics added). Now before you sell your house or put up a fence around your church to keep the people of the world out, I need to tell you what the world is *not* and what it *is*:

- The world we are not to love is not the created order (God created all things).
- The world we are not to love is not the people in the world (we are to love all people).
- The world we are not to love is the world system of evil that offers us sinful desires that destroy our walk with God.

For spiritual children (new believers) it seems out of place to write this after being encouraged to grow in faith. You are in love with God. To you it is obvious that you will never again be in love with the world. At least this is what you think in the beginning. The great pastor Charles Spurgeon wrote about this in his wonderful book *Morning and Evening*. His words are so enlightening to our devotion:

> *At the time of conversion, the conscience is so tender that we are afraid of the slightest sin. Young converts have a holy timidity, a godly fear, lest they should offend God. But very soon the fine bloom on these first ripe fruits is removed by the rough handling of the surrounding world. It is sadly true that even a Christian may grow so callous that the sin which once startled him does not alarm him in the least* (March 11 devotion, 144).

No truer words could come on the heels of John's command "Do not love the world."

If you and I could see the structure of evil put in place by Satan, we would run from it. Our Lord told His apprentices of the wickedness of its leader (John 8:44). Satan's goal is to destroy every believer's effectiveness by engaging him or her in the world system.

I find myself asking John the following question: "John, what is in the world system?" His response is threefold:

- *Sin that attracts the desires of the flesh.* Brothers and sisters, there is sexual perversion on every street corner, in every clothing store, on every TV set, on every smart phone, in every secular song, in every school system, in every college, and in every church.

- *Sin that attracts the desires of the eyes.* The sin described above ties directly to this sin. Someone wrote, "Our eyes are the windows into our heart." It was Samson's eyes that destroyed him. It was Lot's wife's eyes that destroyed her. The list goes on and on. The devil places everything he can get before our eyes. I think of the lure of money that is dangled before a believer's eye to take him or her away from true kingdom life.

- *Sin that attracts the desires of pride.* This world system hides behind the billboard of "Be all you were meant to be." This world system is vicious in attracting its victims in the cesspool of self.

John is pleading with his readers, *Do not love the world.* Now John adds this horrifying truth: *The world is passing away* as humanity is lusting for sin all the way to the grave.

While it is true that Satan cannot steal our souls, he can destroy our effectiveness in this life. By doing so he assures that those in our circle of influence will never see or hear the gospel. This command, "Do not slip," is so important to so many!

In this week's reading you will meet the church at Corinth and discover how Paul confronted them with the very same truth:

Day 1:

Read 1 Corinthians 1–3

and answer the following questions:

- In chapter 2 Paul writes about the "natural man" (NASB). Why is it impossible for the natural man to understand the things of God?
- In chapter 3 Paul refers to our works being judged by God. What works will be burned up when Jesus returns and what will be rewarded?

Day 2:

Read 1 Corinthians 4–6

and answer the following questions:

- As Paul writes about his ministry in chapter 4, it is clear that he has come to poverty for his witness for Christ. Do one's riches hinder or help his or her witness for Christ?

- In chapter 5 we read of a grievous sin in the church. What are some sins of the world that have been accepted in the church?

Day 3:

Read 1 Corinthians 7–9

and answer the following questions:

- Is Paul saying in chapter 7 that it is better to be married or not to be married? Give reasons for your answer.
- In chapter 9 Paul writes about surrendering your rights. What is the world's response to this line of thinking?

Day 4:

Read 1 Corinthians 10–12

and answer the following questions:

- Why did God kill so many people, as described in 1 Corinthians 10? Think through if God is unfair or not, according to 10:10–13.
- According to chapter 12, God has given His people spiritual gifts. Can spiritual gifts be of value in the world system?

Day 5:

Read 1 Corinthians 13–16

and answer the following questions:

- How can I Corinthians 13 help believers to reach people who are in love with the system?
- What effect does the gospel, according to 1 Corinthians 15, have on our lives as Christ-followers in this evil world system? Include 15:58 in your answer.

* * * * * * * *

WEEK SEVEN

The Deception of Our Day
1 John 2:18–27

- - - - - - - -

It was extremely difficult to stay calm as I listened to the couple pour out their hearts to me. I didn't know if it was my zeal for God or my anger at what I was being told. But my heart was angry at what they had endured. The couple had been genuine in their effort to serve the Lord as they had been directed to do. They had trusted their leader to direct them in the correct direction. But now they knew it had been wrong.

I remember crying out to God, "Is this why the church faces such an uphill climb in these last days?" I was truly hurting knowing how the church they had attended had been selling them a bill of goods that said, "You are liberated to do whatever you want to do."

Brothers and sisters, we have been liberated to serve the Lord Jesus Christ. The apostle John has taught us to be liberated from the ways of the world (1 John 2:15–17). We have not been liberated to embrace the ways of the world. This is the deception of our day.

However, there is hope for the church and there is help for those of us who want to serve the Lord in the way He desires. We see this hope and help in the focal text for our week.

John begins this section with a statement: *Children, it is the last hour.*

Those who are students of Scripture know this statement to speak of the age of the church. The prophet Daniel spoke of the hours leading up to his hour (Daniel 9:24–27). Peter wrote about the angels wanting to understand this time (1 Peter 1:12).

John warns us of a last-hour deception: *There are many antichrists.* In the days leading up to the Lord's return there will be many who are false teachers (2 Peter 2:3–7). These teachers are worldly to the core. They are called "antichrists" because they minister in a way that is against Christ.

This is so hard to imagine if you are in a church where the Word of God is faithfully taught. But be assured that our nation is bombarded with leaders who are antichrist. Their number will increase before the second coming of the Lord Jesus. John warns us of their roots being in the church (1 John 2:19). These teachers and pastors come from church backgrounds. But listen carefully—they deviate from the truth they were taught.

John writes, "They went out from us [Jerusalem], but they were not of us [teaching the apostles' doctrine]." See Acts 2:42–44. It has become clear that they are not teaching the truth. They are antichrists.

Today we see the fulfillment of this scripture all around us. There are leaders who say, "It is not important what you believe as long as you believe." This is so untrue and so damning in our world. If I said, "Here is medicine—I think it is good" and you took it and found out it was poison, you would die. While it is true that this is medicine, it is also not true because it is not good medicine.

In this moment, fear could be rising up in you as your wonder who we can trust and who we can believe. This is an honest question in our day of deception. Thankfully John answers the question for us. He informs us of two spiritual "search engine devices" that will see us through to the truth:

- The Holy Spirit

The King James Version uses the phrase "an unction from the Holy One" (1 John 2:20). The word *unction* speaks of charisma. The Lord has anointed His people with the Holy Spirit's discernment. In John 16:13 we are told that the Holy Spirit will guide us into all truth.

We must be certain to pay close attention to the following truth: *Charisma of man is not God's stamp of correctness of a given teaching.* We have been given the Holy Spirit to direct us to truth and to teach truth correctly.

- The Word of God

The apostles' doctrine was clearly taught to the church. The church knew this. If they continued to abide in the Word of God, they would be secure. Brothers and sisters, God's Word is profitable for all things in life (2 Timothy 3:16–17). God's Word must be taught, caught, and lived out in our day.

I want to challenge you to ask God to fill you with the Holy Spirit's anointing to read, heed, and sow His Word this week. I want to challenge you to turn off false teachers. I want to challenge you to leave churches that are false in their teaching. Embrace Bible-believing, Spirit-filled churches that are preaching and living out the Word of God.

Take this week and read each day with a desire to know and practice His Word:

Day 1:
Read 2 Peter 1
and answer the following questions:

- How did the church arrive at having this book called the Bible?
- Can we trust everything the Bible says? Give reasons for your answer.

Day 2:

Read 2 Peter 2

and answer the following questions:

- Why do seemingly true believers embrace false teachers and false teaching?
- What does it mean when the writer says, "The last state has become worse for them than the first" (2 Peter 2:20)? Explain who this refers to.

Day 3:

Read 2 Peter 3

and answer the following questions:

- Why do some people believe Jesus is not coming again?
- What type of people should we be in light of the second coming of Jesus?

Day 4:

Read 2 John 1

and answer the following question:

- What does John mean by "walking in the truth" (v. 4)?
- Why should we not let false teachers in our homes?

Day 5:

Read 3 John

and answer the following questions:

- Why was John so excited about the church walking in the truth?
- Why is there so much corruption in the church, such as false teachers?

* * * * * * * *

WEEK EIGHT

Staying the Course
1 John 2:28–3:3

I ran into an old friend a few years ago I had not seen since our days in seminary. I had often wondered what had happened to him. As we reconnected, the memories came back, and it was as if we had never been apart. We talked about the dreams we had had for our lives. I can recall both of us saying to God, "We want to preach Your Word around the world."

That was twenty-five years ago. There has been much water under the bridge since those days. I remember commenting to my friend, "God has been faithful."

When my friend asked what I had been up to these many years, I was able to say that I had stayed the course with Jesus. I want you to hear this. Days turn into weeks and weeks into months, and ultimately months turn into years. If you are not very committed to staying the course with Jesus, you will waste your life.

Question: Are you staying the course with Jesus?

As we come to a new section in John's writing, we are again given a familiar directive. We have heard this earlier in our studies in 1 John. But as a student of Scripture, you know you have heard it much before the apostle John.

Here is John's familiar directive: *Abide in him*. The NIV translates the word *abide* as "continue." One of the usages of the word is to simply "to stay the course."

Jesus used this word, as recorded by John, seven times in John 15. Here is one of those seven times: "I am the vine; you are the branches. Whoever *abides* in me and I in him, he it is that bears much fruit, for apart from me you can do nothing" (John 15:5, italics added).

God's intention for His "little children" is to continue with Him throughout their lives.

As I talked with my friend, it was clear that he had for a while gotten off the path, but thankfully he had returned. We shared together with great joy, knowing that we were both on the same course for Jesus.

When John encourages us to stay the course, as seen in this week's focal passage, he offers us four amazing reasons to do so. I offer them to you in hopes that if you are *not* on the course, you *will* get on the course with Jesus. I also offer them to you in hopes that if you have gotten *off* the course at some point, you would get *back* on the course. Finally, I offer them to you in hopes that if you are discouraged, these reasons would encourage you. Here are the four amazing reasons to stay the course:

- Someday the Lord will return (v. 28).

We know this day to be that of the Lord's second coming. John, along with the other disciples, had heard Jesus teach this truth (Matthew 24–25). They had heard the angels' promise in Acts 1:11. John for the first time gives us this teaching in 1 John. Later he will be given the vision of the days leading up to the second coming in the book of Revelation.

Why should I stay the course in light of the second coming? When He comes He will reward those who have faithfully served Him (2 Corinthians 5:9–10). John warns us of the consequences of getting off course, noting that there will be shame for those who have lived their lives away from doing what was right. God sees everything now, but when we see Him, we will be reminded of any shame. This is why I want to abide now so I can have confidence when He comes.

- This is what Christians do (v. 29).

Christians stay the course because they are Christians. When one is abiding in Christ, according to Jesus, he or she is bearing fruit of righteousness (John 15:7–10). Just as a person breathes because that is what he or she does for life, so does the person who abides in Christ. We practice righteous living. We are not perfect, but we are progressing in our walk with Christ.

- It is an honor to be a Christian (3:1).

Brothers and sisters, I have never gotten over the fact that God would save such a sinner as me. I cannot climb the heights of His love for such a rebel as me. He has made me His child, and He has given me a place at His table. John is emphatic when he writes, *and so we are.* I am staying the course because it is an honor to follow Jesus. He bought me with a price (1 Corinthians 6:19–20). I want to glorify Him with my life.

- Heaven is worth my all (3:2–3).

The truth is that there is still great mystery when it comes to heaven. There is so much that I do not know. But what I *do* know compels me to want to go. When I get there, I want to see Jesus. Will He will say you and I stayed the course?

For me there is one last footnote in this section of 1 John: "Everyone who thus hopes in him purifies himself as he is pure" (3:3).

As we travel this course in life, the path presents challenges, tests, and temptations. We sometimes get our spiritual clothes dirty. It is in these moments that we have to come back to our source of purity—Jesus. This was the heart of 1 John 1:9. In these moments God cleans us up as we continue to stay the course.

This week I have chosen selected chapters on purifying for you to read. May they encourage you to stay the course:

Day 1:
Read 1 Thessalonians 1
and answer the following questions:
- What types of lifestyles were the people following in this city?
- What effect did the preaching of the gospel have on the people in this city?

Day 2:
Read 1 Thessalonians 2
and answer the following questions:
- What would affectionate care look like in the church today?

- What difficulties did Paul have to endure for his stand for Jesus? In your answer discuss what difficulties we face today.

Day 3:

Read 1 Thessalonians 3

and answer the following questions:

- Why did Paul want this church to stay the course?
- How can we help others stay the course in their spiritual lives?

Day 4:

Read 1 Thessalonians 4

and answer the following questions:

- What does it mean to live a life pleasing to God?
- Why were the people afraid they had missed the second coming of the Lord?

Day 5:

Read 1 Thessalonians 5

- and answer the following questions:
- What will be the signs leading up to the second coming of the Lord?
- How are we to live in light of the second coming?

. . . .

WEEK NINE

People You Wonder About
1 John 3:4–11

F rom my earliest memories, church life has always been a major part of my life. I spent the
first twenty years of my life attending the same country
church. It was there I was introduced to Jesus. It was there
I heard the call of God to salvation. It was there I had my
first kiss. It was there where life happened. It was there
where I formed my worldviews. I owe so much to the
local church.

But there are some things about the church I never
understood. Here is one that is obvious in my memory:
"Why do people always sit in the same places in church?"

I remember where everybody sat. I remember that
the deacons always sat in the back of the sanctuary. The
children were always herded down front, and the families usually sat in the same seats. There was one lady who

always had to have her same spot. I remember when a visitor sat in her spot one Sunday morning. That visitor was never seen again.

Church life can very much become a clique with assigned seating. Honestly, my church was not that way. But there were people in our church I never understood. To this day they remain a great mystery to me. I know what you are thinking--he did not like them because they were from different backgrounds or they were from a different part of the countryside. This really was not the issue.

The issue was simply that they were different. They were people filled with opinions, arguments, evil, and hate. They were the people who always ended up on committees, and they always caused trouble with the people in the church. To me it was obvious: such people were not really a part of God's family. But I had better not say such stuff in front of my momma. My mom used to say, "It's not for you to judge, Keith." I would respond, "The judge is God's Word." But to no avail—our home church remained silent about the people I wondered about.

Was it that they believed God would show those people, or was it that maybe *I* was wrong?

This week John helps us to understand the truth about the people we wonder about. John writes, "By this it is evident." The KJV translates the verse as "By this it is manifested." The NASB translates this as "It is obvious."

It seems as if the New Testament church did not struggle with what was obvious. The church clearly lays out the measurable character traits of people who are the children of God and people who are the children of the devil.

I imagine I would have gotten into some serious trouble if I had walked up to certain people in my home church and addressed them as "children of the devil." But according to John, there are such people in most congregations. So why are we afraid of telling the truth?

The answer may be in this one statement: We really are not sure.

John helps us to be sure. He lists characteristics of both groups. Let me list them for you:

The children of God are
- Those for whom Jesus came to destroy the works of the devil.
- Those from who Jesus took away the power of sin.
- Those for whom Jesus modeled the righteous way of life.
- Those for whom Jesus gave the Holy Spirit as the power behind victorious Christian living.

The children of the devil are
- People who have no connection to Jesus.

- People who have zero change in attitudes and actions.
- People who cannot love those who are not really in their families.

So do you have these people in your church? I have them in the church where I serve. Now, it is true that no one person will be perfect in the church. But each person who is a child of God will be progressing in his or her life as a child of God.

Take time and look at their lives. The pleasure of sin is no longer pleasurable for such a person. Sin no longer is attractive. Sin doesn't taste good, feel good, or look good. It's as if the believer has lost his or her appetite for sin. Such a person is different. One author wrote, "You are habitually different."

I wonder—did my fellow church members get this? I wonder—do people get it today? I always knew that people would never be perfect with each other. But I also knew from the day of God's salvation that I have been a different person, walking with people who also want to be different.

Take time this week to walk with the apostle Paul as he trains a young pastor to lead his church through such a life change:

Day 1:

Read 1 Timothy 1–2

and answer the following questions:

- What are some of the useless discussions churches often get into during business meetings?
- What difference did the gospel make in the way Paul viewed his own life?

Day 2:

Read 1 Timothy 3

and answer the following questions:

- Why does God place fourteen qualifications for the position of pastor? Are any of these obsolete today?
- What would happen if we allowed the qualifications to change?

Day 3:

Read 1 Timothy 4

and answer the following questions:

- Is it harder or easier to be a church member today?
- Why was it so important for Timothy to faithfully teach the Bible?

Day 4:

Read 1 Timothy 5

and answer the following questions:

- Discuss the way each family unit as described in 1 Timothy 5 must function in the church.
- What group has the hardest time fitting into the life of a local church? Give reasons for your answer.

Day 5:

Read 1 Timothy 6

and answer the following questions:

- What is the value of godliness in the life of the church in the twenty-first century?
- What does it mean when Paul says, "Fight the good fight of the faith"? And who is to fight this fight?

* * * * * * * *

WEEK TEN

Authentic Living
1 John 3:11–18

· · · · · · · · ·

As the dust settles from John's evidence locker, we ask ourselves, "Are we truly one of the faithful?" John's desire is not to destroy our confidence but to strengthen our resolve to live an authentic Christian life.

Question: Do you want to be authentic in your life? At my age, more than at any other time in my life, I want to live out what I believe. I want to be who Jesus wants me to be. I am pastoring a church where I see a longing for authentic living. I see other believers hungering for this authentic life.

As we dive into John's next section, we find a familiar statement. It is the second time we are reading this statement. The first time was in 2:7–8. Take a moment and review what you think you remember. Check out chapter four's devotion.

John reminds us of the commandment given by Jesus. This commandment is clear: "Love one another" (John 13:34–35). This is so profound to me today. Each day God gives us new opportunities to authentically live out this command.

John writes, We should love one another (v. 11). The verb *should* is in the present active case, which means we are to be actively loving one another. This is something that requires us to genuinely invest both thought and deed.

We have to think about the person we are to love, and we have to think about why we love him or her. If we fail to actively think through love, we lose the reasons we love, and we end up becoming stale in our love.

In this moment I am thinking about my love for my wife, Sherry. It's easy to actively love her when I think through all of who she is in my life. But my love becomes stale when I take for granted who she is, and I forget all the benefits I have in being married to her.

We also have to invest in deeds of love. When we are thinking correctly, the actions or deeds come naturally. You stop by the grocery for flowers, you pick up your laundry, you leave the note, and you do your best in word and deed to be authentic.

Question: Are you feeling authentic in your love right now?

John offers his readers two warnings when it comes to the commandment of love. Here they are:

- Reject the way of Cain.
- Be ready to be "Cainized."

The story of Cain is familiar to us because of our studies in Scripture. Take a moment and read Genesis 4 to once again become familiar with the story. John answers three questions: 1. Where did Cain come from? 2. What did Cain do? 3. Why did he do it?

Cain could trace his spiritual heritage back to Satan because he was connected to this evil one. He was authentically following the evil way that was in Satan. Cain killed his own brother. His reason, his life was centered in evil deeds.

When life becomes intense, we always reveal what is on the inside! Cain's "What's next" was always worse than what had happened before.

John warns us to be ready to face people like Cain. I call it being "Cainized." The world hates us because their deeds are evil. Such people abide in death. Be careful with these people, because they are even murdering each other. This very day they are moving closer and closer to eternal death.

It's easy for me to love Sherry when I think about her, but it is not so easy to love the world when I think about the world. But I have been called to authentic love with everyone. So what can I authentically do?

John gives insight here. God's love in us changes everything about us. Jesus is the example before us, and His direction is our road map for authentic love. When we love the Jesus way, we begin to give ourselves for others. This authentic living begins to challenge every action of our lives. We no longer just speak about loving others—we are now invested in deeds that evidence our love for one another.

The winds of authentic living fill our spiritual sails with deeds that prove our connection to Jesus. We are no longer people who make empty promises. We are people busy at the work of reaching souls with the gospel.

This week we will spend our studies in the gospel of Matthew. Take the time to allow Scripture to make you more authentic for Jesus.

Day 1:
Read Matthew 5
and answer the following questions:
- What do the Beatitudes reveal about our condition before God?
- In verses 43 through 48, Jesus teaches about loving our enemies. Why is it so hard to love your enemies?

Day 2:

Read Matthew 6

and answer the following questions:

- Why does God have a formula for giving? How can giving become a trap?
- According to verses 22 and 23, did Cain have a good or bad eye to his heart? Explain your answer.

Day 3:

Read Matthew 7

and answer the following questions:

- What requests should we be making to God?
- What kinds of fruit do you want your life to bear?

Day 4:

Read Matthew 8–9

and answer the following questions:

- Who are the lepers in our society and how much love should we have for them?
- Why are we to be praying for laborers in God's work?

Day 5:

Read Matthew 10

and answer the following questions:

- Why do so many people hate each other?
- How does God's love for us give us confidence in a world filled with hate?

WEEK ELEVEN

Living with Assurance
1 John 3:19–24

· · · · · · · · ·

It is with the greatest of joy that I write the following statement of my faith: "I know that I know that I know I am saved." Can you identify with this great joy? Can you rest each night knowing where God is taking you?

John writes of such assurance in this section of his epistle. For those who are living authentic lives, their viewpoint of life is simply this: they are living with assurance. Such people have a confidence in mind and heart about their relationship with God.

Now this might not seem like a big deal to you if you daily have this assurance. But if you do not have it and you want it, it is a big deal. I am personally thinking about three people in particular. The first was a student pastor who came into my office with a genuine look of concern.

He quickly came to his question. He asked, "Do you have any books on your shelves that can help me to come to a place of assurance in my salvation?" The second was a lady who came to my office struggling with which way of life was correct. She could not make up her mind about which path was the best. The third was a lady who had been baptized five times and still was not sure she was right with God.

Each of the above illustrations is close to home to all of us. I want you to know: God does not engage in trickery or in evil by telling a person he or she is saved and then laughing in heaven knowing he or she is not. We have been given His Word as our assurance. In this section of 1 John we find John bringing genuine believers to a place of confidence. There are four questions within this text that help us to come to a place of assurance:

1. What is in your heart?

For many people, the lack of assurance comes from the heart. John writes about our hearts condemning us. The word "condemning" speaks about someone who self-judges, someone who has a very low view of himself or herself. Such a person knows he or she is worthy of blame and always finds fault with himself or herself.

But this person has obeyed the Word of God in confessing and turning from his or her sin. John writes, *God is greater than our heart*. Warren Wiersbe writes, "A 'condemning heart' is one that robs a believer of peace. An 'accusing conscience' is another way to describe it. Sometimes the heart condemns us wrongly. . . . (Jer. 17:9)" (Wiersbe, *The Bible Exposition Commentary*, vol. 1, 129).

God alone knows our hearts, and we must trust what He says about our hearts!

2. In whom is your confidence?

John writes, *we have confidence before God*. The confidence of our salvation must come from God to us. We are called to believe in what He has done (John 10:27–30). We are asked to trust in His keeping power (2 Timothy 1:12). Certainly we do not take sin for granted. But when God has removed sin, we are free indeed.

3. Tell me about your prayer life.

When we are right with God, there is success in our prayer life. However, take note: this is not God's blank check for us to ask and receive anything we want. If our prayers are selfish (James 4:1–2) we will hear a no answer from God. If our prayers are sin-filled, God will not hear (Psalm 66:18).

When we are saved, when we are serving Him, and when we are loving others, our requests come back with the stamp of *yes*! John deals with this even more in 1 John 5:14–15.

One of the reasons I know I am saved is because of answered prayer. I delight to pray the way He wants me to pray (Psalm 37:4).

4. Tell me about your walk.

Often it is someone's lack of a walk with God that fuels his or her doubts and fears. Here John tests our walk. Someone who has a walk with God does three things. First, he or she lives out the very commands of God. This person is keeping the directions of God out of love (John 14:15). Second, he or she loves other people. We have assurance we are God's when we have His love flowing to us, in us, and through us to others. If I am harboring hate, bitterness, and envy in my heart, it could be an indicator of a lack of salvation. Third, he or she is filled with the Holy Spirit. One knows that he or she knows because of God's witness of life inside. The Holy Spirit directs each life that belongs to Jesus (John 16:13–14).

After answering John's questions, I can say with even more confidence, "I know that I know that I know I am saved." I wish I could say all three of the above people came to this place. Two have, and I am praying for the third to come to assurance. I am also praying that this week's assignments will bring greater assurance to you as you study.

Day 1:

Read Psalm 66

and answer the following questions:

- List the things God has done in your life that give you assurance of faith.
- Why does the psalmist give us a warning in verse 18? Explain.

Day 2:

Read Matthew 11

and answer the following questions:

- Why did John the Baptist struggle with doubt? And why do we also do the same?
- What is the "rest" Jesus is referring to in this text?

Day 3:

Read Matthew 12

and answer the following questions:

- What did the Pharisees trust in for their salvation?
- What is blaspheming against the Holy Spirit?

Day 4:

Read Matthew 13

and answer the following questions:

- Why do so many people never understand the Bible?

- According to Jesus (vv. 44–46), how valuable is salvation? Be personal in your answer.

Day 5:

Read Matthew 14

and answer the following questions:

- How would you have responded if people in your hometown rejected Jesus?
- Compare your faith to Peter's. Would you have gotten out of the boat? Explain your answer.

* * * * * * * *

WEEK TWELVE

Truth or Error: How Do We Know the Difference?
1 John 4:1–6

There I sat with two trusted brothers in Christ. We were visiting a church that from the start was very uncomfortable. I had been asked to come, and my two brothers were gracious in attending with me. As soon as the music started I knew I was about to be exposed to things I had never seen or heard. The question on the table for me was this: Is this truth or error? And a second question followed the first closely: "How do I know the difference?"

The apostle Paul gave the church a strong warning about our subject matter when he wrote, "Now the Spirit expressly says that in later times some will depart from the faith by devoting themselves to deceitful spirits and teachings of demons" (1 Timothy 4:1). Was this what I was experiencing, or was I simply uncomfortable because these were third-tier doctrinal differences? Were the people in this place leading others astray, or could it be *I* had been leading people astray?

Brothers and sisters, the above illustration happens every day in our lives. How do we combat such moments and such teaching?

As we come to 1 John 4 it is clear that John is writing about these very things. John begins this chapter with a command: *Do not believe every spirit, but test the spirits to see whether they are from God.*

The word *test* speaks about our attempts to learn the genuineness of something by examination. God has given us His Word as our standard by which we test every teaching of men (2 Timothy 2:15). The previous sentence must become the standard by which you measure truth versus error. Without this standard we fall into the trap of one person's opinion versus another person's opinion.

John gives us shocking truth when he says that you cannot believe every spirit. The word *spirit* is the Greek word *pneuma*, which can be translated as either "Holy Spirit" or "spirit of men" based upon the context. All commentaries agree that this is the spirit of men. John is teaching us how to test the teaching of men. Are the things they say the truth or are they error?

One might ask, "Why is this important?" John's response is clear: *for many false prophets have gone out into the world.* These false teachers have been strategically planted by Satan in the world to lead people astray. This is very scary when we realize that people's souls hang in the balance.

Speaking about the false teachers of His day, Jesus said, "You travel across sea and land to make a single proselyte, and when he becomes a proselyte, you make him twice as much a child of hell as yourselves" (Matthew 23:15). This is not just the pettiness of a Southern Baptist pastor wanting every personal viewpoint to be considered as the Word of God. This is a battle for the truth verses a battle of error with souls hanging in the balance.

John puts before us the test. It is a simple test, but it is very serious:

- If a person openly professes (confesses) Jesus to be the Messiah (come in the flesh), he or she is speaking under the anointing of the Holy Spirit.

The Scriptures make this clear for us. Here are three verses for your consideration: 1 Corinthians 12:3, 1 John 4:15, and 1 John 5:1.

Such people are speaking the Word of God because they hear from God. They *know God.* Such people have come to the knowledge of the truth (1 Timothy 2:2–5). They teach the truth of God revealed in His Word (1 Corinthians 2:11–15). Such people want to partner with others who know God. They together form churches that speak the truth under the anointing of the Spirit of truth.

- If a person does not profess (confess) Jesus to be the Messiah (come in the flesh), he or she is speaking under the power of his or her own spirit or the spirit of Satan (1 Corinthians 12:3).

Now this may seem to be confusing because the natural thought here would be "I don't know anyone who says Jesus did not come in the flesh." Be assured that Mormons and Jehovah's Witnesses do not believe this. And be assured that there are many teachers who fail to understand what it means to confess Jesus as Messiah and Lord. When Jesus becomes your Messiah, you are called to follow His leadership as your Lord. We are to conform our lives to His will. We are to live separated lives (1 Peter 1:13–16).

John MacArthur is correct when he writes, "In the incarnation, God became a partaker of human nature. Through regeneration, on the other hand, human beings become partakers of the divine nature (2 Cor. 3:18)" (*MacArthur New Testament Commentary, 1–3 John*, 158).

Such people, who do not believe Jesus came in the flesh, do not hear from God. But such people often have a large following because they come together with people who are also in darkness. They come together to elevate each other's spirits (2 Timothy 4:2-4). They are each committed because they are under the power of deception being led into delusion by the forces of darkness. The crowd "hears." They accept and pay complete attention to what they are hearing.

Brothers and sisters, we live in a day when people's minds are poisoned by pagan talk show hosts, life coaches, and teachers who were raised with a post-Christian viewpoint—self-appointed apostles and teachers who say, "Thus says the Lord," when they are really are saying, "This is what I believe."

In this moment I want to turn away from those who have the spirit of error. I want you to focus in on *I John 4:4*. For all who are connected to Jesus as their Messiah, each has the Holy Spirit residing within him or her. Such people clearly know the difference between what truth is and what is error. The Spirit gives you what you need in the hour of testing to be able to overcome the error. This very day I am not afraid that I will be taken in by error, and I am not afraid to stand up against those in error because I have the Holy Spirit. And by the way, so do you if you know Jesus as your Messiah.

I pray that our Scripture reading directs us to confidence in our faith as well as inspiration to engage those who are under the delusion of error.

Day 1:

Read Matthew 15

and answer the following questions:

- Why were the teachers of the law living with hearts far from God? Compare this to our day in your answer.
- What is the only thing that can change a person's heart? Give examples from your own life.

Day 2:

Read Matthew 16

and answer the following questions:

- Why did the people want more signs from Jesus? What types of signs are many churches performing today?
- Why did Peter confess Jesus as the "Christ"? What does this mean to you personally?

Day 3:

Read Matthew 17

and answer the following questions:

- What does it mean when Jesus said, "They did to him whatever they pleased"?
- If we have mustard seed faith, then why are not more mountains being moved?

Day 4:

Read Matthew 18

and answer the following questions:

- Why did Jesus use a child for His illustration of true greatness? Where do you see people who have childlike faith?
- How do verses 7 through 9 serve as a warning to modern-day false teachers?

Day 5:

Read Matthew 19

and answer the following questions:

- What does the Bible truly teach about marriage, divorce, and remarriage?
- What was the rich young ruler's problem?

* * * * * * * *

WEEK THIRTEEN

A Love Like His
1 John 4:7–17

As we come to our next section of 1 John it is good to remember this fact: "The Spirit of truth at work in the believer causes a total personal makeover in his or her life." I know this for real because I have seen it countless times in my Christian life.

I recall meeting a classmate after many years. He recognized me and quickly called my name from across the way from where I was shopping with my parents. As he approached, I did not recognize him until he told me his name. As soon as he spoke his name, my mind went back to my high school days and the very last time I had seen him. I wondered what had happened in the years between our seeing each other. In a very short conversation I recognized something amazing had happened in his life. Joy filled my heart as he told me the story of his meeting Jesus.

Brothers and sisters, when the Spirit of truth is at work in us, we are not only acting differently—we *are* different! The difference is the love of God flowing through our lives. Throughout our study John has taught us over and over about this love. With each new section our understanding of this love grows deeper and deeper. This love according to 4:7 flows from God because He is the God of love.

As I write this devotion I am sitting on my office couch with tears flowing and silent praises going up before this loving and holy God. I feel God's love so strongly on my life. All God's blessings have come to me not because I am worthy of them, not because I have earned them. They have come because He is a loving God.

Sitting here, I long for one thing in this moment. You ask, "What are you longing for?" My answer: I want to have a love like His. It is what I need to do ministry in the 21st century. It is what I need to do ministry in my family and my church. I say it again: I want to have a love like His.

Oh, how I hope you want the same thing today! In the section before us, John teaches us how to have a love like His. John accomplishes this task by doing the following:

- John places the principle of love before us in verses 7–8.

This principle is so profound: "God is love." Everything you could possibly want to know about unconditional love is found in God. Unless you and I understand this principle and accept it, we can never love as He loves.

God's consistent command throughout this epistle has been "Love one another." We know we are saved when we love as He loves. Can you see the flow of love? It originates from the living water of God's heart flowing down into those who have received this living water. It then flows from their stream into the brook of other people's lives. God never intends for it to be dammed up. God's love is intended to flow. Yes, He wants us to love like Him.

- John gives us proof of God's love in verses 9–10.

This is where I want to stop writing and lift my hands in strong praise—because the proof is in the incarnation and the cross of Jesus Christ. God sent His only Son to this world. Wayne Grudem writes in *Systematic Theology*:

> *God the Father agreed to give the Son to people He would redeem for His own possession (John 17:2, 6). He prepared a body for the Son to dwell in as a man (Colossians 2:9). He agreed to accept Him as representative of His people whom He would redeem (Hebrews*

9:24). God the Son agreed to come and live as a man under the Mosaic Law (Galatians 4:4) and be perfectly obedient to the Father's commands, unto death on a cross (Philippians 2:8) (Wayne Grudem, *Systematic Theology*, 518-19).

Brothers and sisters, do we need any more proof?

- John reveals the purpose of God's love in verses 11–12.

God has set the standard of love before us so that we would love in the same way He loves. As we mature in loving God and in loving others, His love is shown in full expression. It becomes perfected as we love the way He loves.

- In verses 13–17 John reminds us of the power we have that makes love happen.

Each day the witness of the Holy Spirit reminds us to love one another. Each day the Holy Spirit gives us power to tear down everything that robs us of the free flow of love (2 Corinthians 10:3–5). Each day the Holy Spirit directs us to clearly confess of God's love for us, in us, and working through us. I would never have a love for others unless He was filling me with His love.

In verse 16 we are reminded that there is really no love in this world that could ever compare to His love for us. Brethren, this love is beyond our ability to explain it all. But it is not beyond our ability to grasp personally for our own lives.

As I talked with my old classmate, I realized that we were now in a different place because of the love of God poured out in our lives. As I left our conversation I was glad the love of God was flowing. I wondered, "Did he see the love of God flowing from my life?" After all these years I still want to have a love like His!

It is my prayer that as we examine this week's readings we would increase in a love like His.

Here are our readings for the week:

Day 1:

Read Matthew 20

and answer the following questions:

- How has God's love affected you in the area of generosity to others?
- How can God's love flow through you in ways that would lead you to serve others with a loving heart?

Day 2:

Read Matthew 21

and answer the following questions:

- Was it out of love that the people praised Jesus when He came to the city? Explain.
- Why did Jesus cleanse the Temple? Was it out of love? Explain.

Day 3:

Read Matthew 22

and answer the following questions:

- Why do so many people easily reject God's love?
- According to verses 34–40, the commandments are summarized in two principles. Which of the principles is hardest for you?

Day 4:

Read Matthew 23

and answer the following questions:

- Why did the religious leaders do their works in front of others? Explain.
- According to verse 27, the people were dead on the inside. How could the love of God have changed them on the inside?

Day 5:

Read Matthew 24

and answer the following questions:

- Why will the love of many grow cold in the days leading up to the tribulation?
- How does the truth of verses 29–31 affect your love for Christ?

* * * * * * * *

WEEK FOURTEEN

The Confidence of Love
1 John 4:17–21

I really did not know if I could continue our friendship. In years gone by I had held great confidence in
our friendship, but now I was not so sure. Fourteen years
of good times and not-so-good times had taken their toll
on my confidence level in our friendship. So I did the only
thing I knew I could do: I put the "For Sale" sign on our
family vehicle.

Yes, you read the previous sentence correctly. I had
a great friendship with our family vehicle. For all those
years I trusted my wife and kids into its sure passage
from place to place. But now things had changed. Question: Are there areas in your life where your confidence is
wearing thin?

As John writes to the church, we read of a God whose
love for us can be completely trusted. He is a God who

is always reaching out to us in love. Remember John's words from chapter 3: *By this we know love, that he laid down his life for us* (v. 16). We are called to love others as He loved us. As we complete chapter four in our studies, John is still on this theme.

Here is our thesis tying all John has written under the inspiration of Scripture: If God's love is in you (you have it), if God's love is increasing in you (growing in you), and if God's love is flowing through you (you're giving it to others), you can be confident in your Christian life."

The confidence of God's love can be seen in three distinct parts of your Christian life:

1. In the reality of your *maturing* in Christ.
2. In the reality of your *meeting* the Lord at death or in the second coming.
3. In the reality of your becoming *more* and *more* like Christ each day.

The more God's love is at work, the more confidence we have in the Christian life. In 4:17 the English Standard Version uses the word "confidence." However, the King James Version uses the word "boldness." I love the New Living Translation, which says, "not afraid . . . but we can face him with confidence." It is true the Lord will someday return (2:28; 3:2; Acts 1:11; Colossians 3:4; Philippians 3:21). You and I do not have to fear meeting the Lord nor do we have to fear the world or the people in it. We do not have to fear the flesh taking charge of our lives. Even when we fail, the love of God overcomes our failure.

Do you know what fear is like? Fear is the opposite of confidence. The Greek word suggests being in severe distress, aroused by intense concern for impending pain, danger, evil, or possibly the illusion of such circumstances.

When God's love is maturing in your life, you will *cast out fear.* I can honestly say that as I have grown in my confidence in God's love, I have watched as God has removed, silenced, driven out, and done away with more and more fears in my life.

Brothers and sisters, have confidence in God. Speak to your enemy and tell him that he no longer has authority over you, your home, your family, your present, or your future. Fear is like punishment. The King James Version uses the word *torment.*

When we are in fear, we are being tortured mentally, which wears on us physically. In your body, mind, and spirit you feel the pain. But this is not what God intends for your life. He wants you to have confidence. Remember 2 Timothy 1:7—"God hath not given us the spirit of fear; but of power, and of love, and of a sound mind" (KJV). In His love God has adopted you into His family (Romans 8:15–16).

If you are living in fear, God's love has not been perfected yet! But there is good news: God has not lost confidence in you as His child. He is still working in you and through you (Philippians 1:6). You are on the path, and be assured that there will never be a "For Sale" sign placed over your life.

Look at I John 4:19. It was God who loved us first, so our love toward Him is secondary to His unconditional love for us. You and I would have never experienced true love apart from Him. Others would not be experiencing your true love apart from Him. So we press into His love.

As John closes the chapter on the subject of love, he gives us a final test and testimony concerning love: verses 20–21. If we say, "I love God," we must also love others. However, if we say, "I love God," but also "I hate my brother," we are lying. The word *hate* can be translated in one of the following ways: *dislike, detest, despise*, or *wish death upon*.

John is teaching us of the impossibility of being in love with God while hating those around us. If we cannot love those we see, how can we love God, whom we cannot see? Such a person has no confidence in this life or the life to come. His or her life is totally a counterfeit. This person is totally confused and is facing the wrath of God.

But praise God—this is not what awaits us. We have the command of God to both grow in His love and to give

His love to others. As you prepare to walk through this week's reading plan, ask yourself, "Do I live in fear and hate?" Confess your answers to God, and seek to obey God's directions for your life.

This week in our readings we will see God's love in the cross.

Day 1:

Read Matthew 25

and answer the following questions:

- Was God unloving in not waiting for the virgins to get more oil for their lamps? Consider in your answer God's directions to them before the night of His coming.
- According to verses 31–40, how does love play into how we treat those around us?

Day 2:

Read Matthew 26

and answer the following questions:

- Why did Mary give Jesus the most expensive thing she had?
- What role did Jesus' love for us have in His prayer in the garden?

Day 3:

Read Matthew 27

and answer the following questions:

- How does the crucifixion of Jesus affect your love for Him and people around you?
- Why did Joseph of Arimathea offer his cemetery plot to Jesus? What of great value have we offered to Jesus?

Day 4:

Read Matthew 28

and answer the following questions:

- In verse 10, why were the women afraid?
- When we read the Great Commission in Matthew 28, we find ourselves being directed to take the gospel to the entire world. Why has it taken almost two thousand years to complete the task?

Day 5:

Read Acts 1

and answer the following questions:

- Why did the apostles stand gazing up into heaven in Acts 1:10? Does it sometimes seem as if the church is *gazing* instead of *going* today? Give reasons in your answers.
- Why was it important for the church to put the failure of Judas behind them?

WEEK FIFTEEN

Overcoming Faith
1 John 5:1–15

In my early days of ministry I found myself often struggling with overcoming faith. Part of my struggle was with bad theology. I grew up in a church that stayed away from anything that would come close to being Pentecostal. If anyone even suggested overcoming faith apart from salvation, he or she was labeled as liberal. But at the same time, part of my struggle was bad practices. My grandmother was fully engaged in the Pentecostal moment of her day. I would occasionally attend church with her. In those services there were always those moments when we were told to name it and receive it. I tried it several times, and as John Wayne once said, "I came up with an empty faith sack."

Bad theology and bad practices led me to live confused in the early years of my faith. I had very little overcoming faith. But then I was exposed to John's teaching. Chapter 5 particularly brought me to a liberating place where now by His grace I live in overcoming faith.

It is my prayer that 1 John 5 will lead you to overcoming faith.

The first word of chapter 5 offers each of us hope because the word *everyone* speaks about a special group of people. These people have each done the following:

- They have believed that Jesus is both man and God. He is their Messiah.
- They have been born of the Father, and they love the Father.
- They are joyously obeying the commandments of God.

The outworking of such a life is *victory over the world*. Keep in mind that *world* here is a reference to the evil world system directed by Satan. Can you say with truthfulness, "I have victory over the world"?

To have victory speaks of conquering and defeating evil. This is an amazing proposition in life, but the question arises: "Do we conquer in our power, or is the power from an outside source?" John says, the victory is achieved *by faith*.

Now this is where it gets clouded for many people. There are people I meet who fall into one of the following categories in their response to the question. Some respond, "I've tried this, but I had no success." Some respond, "I'm afraid to try." Others respond, "I like being in charge of my life, so I don't let go." Others stay away from even thinking about faith. Finally, there are those who by faith overcome the world.

I don't know which group you are in, but the "everyone" in verse one is the group that I am in. I have discovered that overcoming faith is centered not in me or my efforts but in Jesus Christ. The three points above are all "by faith" actions taken by those who have conquering faith.

Let's drill down deeper on the above points.

First, when a person believes in Jesus, he or she is believing that Jesus is trustworthy in who He says He is. He is fully human. As a human being He did the following: He represented us; He became our substitute (Hebrews 2:16–17); He became our mediator (1 Timothy 2:5); He became our example and pattern in life. He is also fully God (deity). Only God could pay the price for our sin (2 Corinthians 5:21). Salvation is of the Lord (Jonah 2:9).

This is where victory begins. He is our overcoming Savior and Lord.

Second, when a person believes that he or she is born again by God, God the Father becomes our Father. We are now the Father's children (Romans 8:13–17). We know He cares for us, protects us, and provides for us in this life (Psalm 138:6–8). He has birthed us to new life, and we love Him (Luke 11:1).

This love we have for Him leads us to love all the Father's children. This is not a natural process—it is a spiritual process for those who are born again and growing in their new lives. This is overcoming faith.

Last, we joyously obey the commandments of God. Here is where true victory evidences itself. Warren Wiersbe wrote, "Everything in creation except humanity obeys the will of God" (*The Bible Exposition Commentary,* vol. 1, 333). Men obey God only when they have faith in God. "By faith" changes everything in your life.

Now you seek to do His will by obeying His commandments. His commandments become a delight to your life. They are not a burden or "grievous" (KJV). God has given His Word as the road map for daily victory in a world filled with traps. His Word is truly "a lamp to my feet and a light to my path" (Psalm 119:105). Suddenly the Word becomes extremely important to your life. Before your conversion, reading the Word was a "have to," but now it is a "get to." Before, the Word was a "made to," and now it is a "want to." Before you were a jerk in fighting the truth of God, but now you are joyously keeping His commandments.

In all these things you suddenly realize that the battle is the Lord's (Exodus 14:13–15; Job 2:9; 1 Corinthians 15:54–58; Revelation 7:10). I want you to know that we get to be conquerors by faith. So I tell you that it's by faith that we have victory in the world. I wrote the following when I had finished feasting on John's writing:

> *Many people who profess to believe live lives in which they are really puppets of the world! They live under the thumb of the world system (5:19). Each week they profess to be changing and charging hell, but each week they are clinging to a world system that controls their every move. All the while a dusty Bible is lying by their bed and a cobweb-filled prayer room is not being used. Each week they want others to believe they have conquering faith, but they are really conquered, because they don't have faith.*

This week our Scripture reading is from a command-filled book, the book of James. You will be challenged each day to have conquering faith.

Day 1:
Read James 1
and answer the following questions:

- How can obeying God's Word keep you from falling into the trap of temptation? Consider verses 12–18 in your answer.
- According to verse 22, we are to be "doers of the word." List some reasons people fail to be doers of God's Word.

Day 2:

Read James 2

and answer the following questions:

- When James writes about partiality in verses 1–13, how does it make you feel? Do you long to do it right? Explain.
- What role does work play in one's faith?

Day 3:

Read James 3

and answer the following questions:

- How does conquering faith lead us to have victory over the tongue?
- How do you receive God's wisdom according to verses 13–18?

Day 4:

Read James 4

and answer the following questions:

- How does worldliness rob you of power in your walk with God?
- In verses 13–17, how does faith in God's sovereign plan lead you to rejoice?

Day 5:

Read James 5

and answer the following questions:

- What role does patience have in your faith life?
- Describe your prayer life as a conquering Christian.

* * * * * * * *

WEEK SIXTEEN

Easter: Where Real Life Begins
1 John 5:6–12

As I write this devotion, Easter has just passed. Here at First Baptist Church of Jackson, Georgia, we had record crowds for our weekend services. For me personally it was a very special weekend in getting to share with hundreds of people the message of Easter.

Usually Easter is the most attended service of the year, with a measurable drop-off the next week. But this year was different: many of those folks came back the next week as a testimony of their belief that Easter changes everything.

The apostle John would say Easter is where real life begins.

You and I have been studying the epistle of 1 John together for fifteen weeks. Just last week we read of the overcoming of the world that faith we can have in and through Jesus!

One year has passed since the previous Easter, and as you read this devotion, Easter has come once again. Easter is about the moment when the Son of God, who had come as the Son of man, would go to the cross to purchase our forgiveness of sins and our right standing before a holy God.

John teaches us of the real life we have if we believe Jesus did these things and is the Son of God.

The verses in our focal text are so rich with truth concerning what we are to believe about Jesus. Pay close attention here: Having believed, we have life in Him. For those of you who do not believe, pay closer attention. If you do not believe, you will not have eternal life.

John sets out to both convince us of this truth and to compel those who do not believe to believe. Here is John's thesis: Jesus is the Christ, who is the Son of God. Eternal life is received only through belief in Him. I write this again: This is where real life begins.

Notice John's proof. He writes, "This is he who came by water and blood." What in the world is John making reference to? Some people believe he is referring to John 19:34, when the solider pierced Jesus' side at the cross and water and blood came out. These people believe it is John's way of saying, "Look to the cross for your proof."

While this is true, I believe along with many others that John is referring both to Jesus' baptism (water), when the Father gave witness to Jesus being His beloved Son (Matthew 3:13–17), and to the blood of the cross on which Jesus died (Ephesians 1:7).

John also makes reference to the Spirit of truth. We know this to be the Holy Spirit who has been given (John 15:27) to convince us of who Jesus is. How does the Holy Spirit do this? Here are four ways He convinces us of who Jesus is:

- He illuminates our minds through the Word of God (1 Corinthians 2:4; 2 Peter 1:19–21; John 5:36–47).
- He speaks through His people—Christians (Acts 1:8; John 15:17; 1 John 1:1–5).
- He speaks through personal conviction from God (John 16:9–11).
- He speaks through the miracles of people's changed lives (Titus 2:12; 2 Corinthians 5:17; Ephesians 4:17–24).

Jesus' baptism, His cross, and the Holy Spirit all agree that it is true: Jesus is the Son of God, who alone gives eternal life. It is true: God has written down in His Word the true record of Jesus.

In verse 10 we are reminded that we who are believers have the true record within us. This is our testimony. Yes, it is true that you and I were not there two thousand years ago to give a firsthand account of Easter. But we know it was all true because we see the evidence of Easter in our lives each day. I have experienced the power of God in changing my life. I see it in the changed lives of others.

Question: Is John's proof enough for you? This question has eternal implications. True life begins when you believe this, or true life continues to escape you if you do not believe.

Two realities for those who do not believe:

- They make God a *liar*.

This does not mean, of course, that God is a liar. It means in their lives they believe God is lying. It also means they will influence others to believe Jesus is lying.

- They are rejecting their only *hope*.

Jesus came to give me life (Mark 10:45). Life is in His name. This life begins here, and it continues for eternity. One unknown author wrote, "If you are thinking 'eternal life' is simply living forever as you presently are, you are missing the point."

Brothers and sisters, I want to be changed. I want to be without sin. I want to be without pain, heartache, sorrow, and the flesh. This reality is what eternal life gives only to those who believe. If a person does not believe, he or she will never have life here or in the hereafter. For such people, eternity will be hell under the wrath of God.

But to those who believe, true life has come and will continue for all eternity. I rejoice with the brethren in celebrating this true life!

This week's assignments:

Day1:

Read Revelation 20

and answer the following questions:

- What will heaven be like?
- How different is heaven from life on the earth now and hell in eternity?

Day 2:

Read Revelation 21

and answer the following questions:

- Why will God not let just anyone into heaven?
- What will be the most precious thing in heaven for you personally?

Day 3:

Read Revelation 22

and answer the following questions:

- What type of light does Jesus give off, according to verses 5–6?

- Does the prospect of Jesus' soon coming change anything in your viewpoint of life? Give examples.

Day 4:

Read Romans 1

and answer the following questions:

- Why would any believer be ashamed of the gospel? Explain where you stand in sharing the gospel.
- Why does God reveal His wrath from heaven?

Day 5:

Read Romans 2

and answer the following questions:

- How can God's kindness lead to someone's repentance?
- What purpose does the law serve in God's judging of all men?

* * * * * * * *

WEEK SEVENTEEN

God's Assurance on Paper
1 John 5:13–17

I have so enjoyed our devotions together in 1 John. Each week I have been convinced of the following: John has never once had a hidden agenda or a secret meaning in his writings. He has been writing under the inspiration of the Holy Spirit (2 Peter 1:18–21). His goals have been consistent throughout our study:

1. He desires unbelievers to believe.
2. He desires believers to have assurance of faith.

These themes are much on his mind as he continues to write in verse 13. He is putting onto paper God's assurance to all men who believe in Jesus.

Now I know the above sentence may not seem important to some who read this. I can hear from my past the words of my grandfather, who said to a customer who had failed to pay his debt, "The signature you placed here promising to pay your debt is not worth the paper it is written on."

Be assured: it is not that way with God. John is essentially saying, "I am writing to you who are in God's family. We are brethren because you believed in the Son of God, and I have believed in the Son of God." This title, "Son of God," speaks to Jesus being the heavenly eternal Son who is equal to God himself (Matthew 11:25–30; 17:5; 1 Corinthians 15:28; Hebrews 1:1–13). John has proven to us who Jesus is. All who believe in Him have life in His name (John 20:31).

In this section of John's writing we are brought to assurance of faith. It is right before us on paper, the paper being God's Word.

God's Word gives us four eternally important items:

- God's Word gives us a *calling* to faith.

From its first page to its last page, this Bible gives us the calling to believe on the Lord Jesus Christ for our salvation (Acts 16:31). In the book of Revelation we are called to come to Jesus (Revelation 22:17).

- God's Word gives us *clarity* of faith.

In 1 Corinthians 2:10–13 we are told that God opens our eyes to the truth and gives us the Holy Spirit as the illuminator of who He is and what He says to us in His Word. Through the Holy Spirit we have the mind of Christ.

- God's Word gives us *certainty* of faith.

John writes, "that you may know." God carries you to the knowledge of the truth. A realization has come. Everything God says is true. I came to this certainty in February 1974. Since then I have kept believing (1 John 5:13), and I will keep on believing, because I am certain of His Word.

- God's Word gives us a *confident* faith.

Our confidence is not in ourselves but in Him. We can rely on Him because He is dependable and faithful. We can always come before Him (vv. 14–15) with boldness of faith in prayer (Hebrews 4:14–16). We do not have to be afraid to talk with Him.

When we pray (as Christ-followers) we pray knowing two things:

1. The will of God

This is so amazing to me. Christ-followers have access to God in a way nonbelievers do not. We have accountability with God through confession (John 9:31; 15:17; Psalm 66:18). We align with God through praying in His will. We get what we ask because it is God's will (John 14:13–14).

2. The work of God

Prayer is truly work. When we petition God, we are engaged in intercessory prayer. In verses 16 and 17 we see an illustration of this. We are called to pray for believers who commit sin not leading to death. These are brothers and sisters who are under God's chastening hand because of some sin. We pray for their repentance, God's mercy, and His restoration.

But there are brothers and sisters we are not to pray for. These are those who decide to walk away from God. They are committing willful sin that they refuse to confess or turn from. God is about to take drastic action.

God wants every believer to pick up His Words on paper daily. He wants us to respond to its call. He wants us to allow the Word to clarify our daily lives. He wants to bring us to a place of assurance in His Word. Ultimately He wants us to intercede on behalf of our brothers and sisters. I hope you will be challenged this week as your read God's Word to have assurance.

This week's assignments:

Day 1:

Read Romans 3

and answer the following questions:

- According to verses 9 through 18, how many people enter this world without sin? A follow-up question would be—how many people have access to Christian prayer from their first day on the earth?

- Why was it important for Jesus to be both God and man? Focus in on verses 23–26.

Day 2:

Read Romans 4

and answer the following questions:

- How did Abraham come to a place of forgiveness before God?

- How does Abraham's testimony enlighten our lives?

Day 3:

Read Romans 5

and answer the following questions:

- What does it mean to you personally to have peace with God?

- When did your salvation begin? Was it with you or before you? Explain.

Day 4:

Read Romans 6

and answer the following questions:

- According to verse 12, what does sin reigning in your body mean?
- How do verses 12–14 help you form your intercession for fellow believers? Explain.

Day 5:

Read Romans 7

and answer the following questions:

- Explain what Paul means by "the new way of the Spirit" in verse 6.
- Do believers struggle with sin after salvation? Use Paul's teaching in verses 13 through 25 in your answer.

* * * * * * * *

WEEK EIGHTEEN

Knowing What You Know
1 John 5:18–21

For the past eighteen weeks you and I have been reading God's Word together. Each week we have been feasting on the Word of God, which has brought us to a greater understanding of who God is and what He desires for our lives. Here are three things we have come to know during these weeks:

1. We have come to know Jesus, who is our Lord and Savior, in a deeper way. He has caused us to be born again (5:18).
2. We have come to have an anointing from the Holy Spirit to understand (2:27) who Jesus is and how we are to live our lives.
3. We have come to a deeper commitment to our faith, our deeds, and our work.

These are wonderful eternal truths that center us for the task of living out our Christian faith. However, there is more. We see one last paragraph in the letter written by John. Three times John writes, *We know.*

John is not being arrogant about a superior knowledge. He is writing to warn us to stay focused on knowing what we know. The Bible over and over instructs us to be careful never to wander away from what we know is true. Those who truly progress and cross the finish line keep God's Word in front of them. The cry of the psalmist comes to mind:

> *Let my cry come before you, O LORD; give*
> *me understanding according to your*
> *Word! (Psalm 119:169).*

As John concludes his letter to us, we find five reminders of things we know and should always know:

1. We know everyone born of God does not *keep* on sinning (v. 18).

This truth is something that you and I (First Baptist Church of Jackson) know very well, but does the church in America know this? Do the churches in the world understand this? The King James Version stresses the importance of this even more with its translation "sinneth not." The New Living Translation translates these words as follows: "do not make a practice of sinning."

John is not reminding us to be perfect, which cannot be attained this side of heaven (1 John 1:6–9). John is reminding us of the change that comes when we are "born again." We no longer want to indulge in a sinful lifestyle. We no longer enjoy sin. We long to walk in holiness.

2. We know everyone born of God seeks to *obey* God's commands (v. 18).

Even though this is not written here in the text, it is assumed by the weight of John's writing for five chapters and from the weight of the entire Bible. The believer is keeping the commandments of God (Psalm 119:9).

3. We know everyone born of God is *protected* by God (v. 19).

We serve an amazing God, who has our back and has our front as well. He watches over our lives. The one "born of God" here is a reference to Jesus Christ. He is the door of the sheepfold, and it is He who protects us from the wickedness of Satan's attacks. Check out John 10:9–18. All I can say is "Wow!"

Satan is identified here as *the evil one*. I researched this and discovered that Satan is the one who personifies evil. Evil originated with him. Satan comes daily against the people of God. His desire is to *touch* our lives. The word "touch" speaks about doing harm to us in no fewer than three ways: physical, moral, and spiritual. We ask ourselves, what does this look like?

- Satan physically puts traps in our lives identified as lusts of the flesh (2:15–16).
- Satan morally puts traps in our lives identified as sexual perversions of all kinds (Romans 1:18–32).
- Satan places spiritual traps in our lives identified as idols (5:21). These idols come to take the place of God in our hearts.

There is great fear in knowing this. However, if you know and follow Jesus, the fear is removed (Luke 12:5; Titus 2:12). We have His promise of victory (4:4). True believers walk around the traps of Satan (Psalm 119:105).

4. We know everyone not born of God is in the *trap* of the evil one (v. 19).

The evil one has a system filled with traps. This system is called the world. Jesus came into this world to save sinners (1 Timothy 1:15). The cross changes everything for those who come to Jesus (Galatians 6:14). Christians are called to shine as lights in this world system (Philippians 2:15).

Imagine being back in the world. Oh, how tragic it is! Every person is in the trap. Some people know this, but they cannot get out. However, many do not know they are in the trap. Still there are others who want to stay in the trap. Jesus came to rescue such people from the trap (Isaiah 61:1; 2 Corinthians 4:4–6).

So many around us are hooked on the world system, on the spiritual cocaine of the world's self-indulgence. Men cannot pull away on their own. Men will not pull away from what they are pursuing (2 Peter 2:22).

Ours is the task of showing them what we know and sharing with them what we know. Verse 20 is a strong reminder of what we know.

5. We know that everyone born of God keeps himself or herself away from *idols* (v. 21).

Keep in mind that idols take the place of the things we know because our eyes focus on new things. John MacArthur writes, "Anything that people elevate above God is an idol of the heart. Every 'lofty thing raised up against the knowledge of God' (2 Corinthians 10:5) must be smashed, and only Christ exalted" (*MacArthur New Testament Commentary, 1–3 John*, 210).

True followers of Christ must look toward what they know to be true in order to know what is not true. I want to encourage you to consider Psalm 119:9–11 in charting a path around idols.

I am so glad we have walked this journey together. May we always be reminded to know what we know. This week's reading assignments will increase what we know.

This week's assignments:

Day 1:

Read Romans 8

and answer the following questions:

- How does an accurate knowledge of God and His Word help you to combat the condemning reminders of your past?
- According to verse 12, what debt do we owe God? Give examples.

Day 2:

Read Romans 9

and answer the following questions:

- Why did Paul have such sorrow in his heart for those who did not believe in Jesus? Include in your answer how you feel about such people.
- Explain God's sovereign choices and humanity's responsibility.

Day 3:

Read Romans 10

and answer the following questions:

- What does Paul ask us to do in verses 9 and 10? Clue for your answer: the gospel is here.

- What steps do you have to take personally to share the gospel?

Day 4:

Read Romans 11

and answer the following questions:

- According to verses 9 and 10, Israel fell into both a snare and a trap. Explain what they were in your own words.

- What does it mean to be "grafted" into God's family? Are you grafted in?

Day 5:

Read Romans 12

and answer the following questions:

- Why is it so important for both your mind and body to be surrendered to God?

- List the marks of a Christian given by Paul in this chapter. Make a chart and place a check by the ones you are doing and a star by the ones you need to work on.

* * * * * * * *

WEEK NINETEEN

The Impact of Truth
2 John 1:1–6

A s we turn the page to our next devotion, we discover that we are looking at a new letter. The name in the top left-hand corner of the letter says it is from "the *elder*." This term is familiar to us in a different context. In our culture we use the word to speak about someone who has come to the later years of his or her life. But in biblical times the word was used to speak about one who was in the place of accepted authority.

The apostle John was correctly identifying himself as an elder. Peter speaks of true pastors using the identification of "elder" in 1 Peter 5:1–2. This elder is addressing his letter to *the elect lady*.

There are varying opinions about who this person is. Could this be a reference to the church as it is sometimes called in the New Testament: "the bride of Christ"?

I personally believe John is writing to a lady who had been chosen by God to be saved and to have a church in her home.

John's letter to her, and to the church in her home, has two clearly defined purposes:

- John wanted the church to continue to position themselves in loving obedience to God's commands.
- John wanted the church to beware of those who were spreading false teaching. His writing is a clear direction of how to respond to such people.

As I studied this one-chapter book, I thought, "I can put this in one devotion." But the longer I studied, the deeper and wider the truth of this book became. I know I would be robbing you of the great truth of this book if I limited it to one devotion.

So I have broken down the study into John's clearly defined purposes. This week we will study together the impact of truth, and next week we will study John's strong warning in the words "Watch yourselves" (v. 8).

John begins his letter by expressing strong words of devotion to this lady in verse 1: *whom I love in truth.* As we know from previous studies in 1 John, the word *love* speaks of a close affection of the heart generated by a love for God that translates into a love for other people.

Jesus is the embodiment of truth (John 14:6). All truth comes from Him. Jesus implants that truth into all who receive Him as Lord and Savior (James 1:18). We are different people because of the impact of truth.

Question: Have you been impacted by the truth? Those who make up the church will be engaged in loving each other in and through the truth. We are called to center ourselves in love and to show honor to those we love (Romans 12:10). When a person comes to know the truth of God's great love, he or she is changed on the inside, which then leads to an outward change.

Someone once said, "Oh, give him six-months and he'll be back to his old ways." John says just the opposite: this truth will abide in this person for all eternity. Certainly, we will fail in loving always, but God's grace, mercy, and peace will see us through these tough moments.

John had received news that many in this house church were walking in this very truth. They were followers of Jesus. John was overjoyed by this, just as any elder would be in seeing his church walk in truth.

In verses 5–7 John points this church to two imperatives that have great impact in us:

1. You must continue to grow in your love.

Brothers and sisters, sometimes we forget this. John has already encouraged us to do this in 1 John 2:7–11.

Here we see it in context of something they should already know. Over and over Jesus taught this truth to His church leaders (John 13:34–35). The love is there implanted in you, but you have to intentionally cultivate it. Hebrews 10:24 says, "Let us consider how to stir up one another to love and good works."

Each day I have to be intentional to cultivate this truth. My old nature wants to be mean, selfish, condemning, judgmental, and downright hateful. But God's implanted truth speaks up through the conviction of the Holy Spirit and reminds me of truth. This truth moves me to grow in love—but not only in love, for there is so much more the Lord has for me.

2. You must continue to grow in living out his commandments.

In verse 6 John writes about how we demonstrate keeping His commandments by the way we love. God's Ten Commandments each are demonstrated by the impact of love. For example, my father is getting up in years. Each day, seven days a week, I call him in the morning. Some days we go back over what we talked about the day before. But I do it every day because I want to obey the commandment "Honor your father and your mother."

Let's try one more: "You shall not murder." It is God's truth of love that leads me to be kind to those who cut me off in traffic instead of flipping them off. It is God's commandment that says to honor all of life.

Following God's commandments is a truth deal that directs us not only on Sundays but every other day of the week was well. It's not only when I am on a mission trip that I have a heart for the hurting—it's right here at home too.

As you and I consider this week's reading assignments, the words of John fill our minds and hearts: *you should walk in it* (God's commandment).

This week's reading assignments:

Day 1:
Read Romans 13
and answer the following questions:
- How does Paul's teaching lead us to treat our political leaders? Explain.
- Why does Paul teach us that we owe love to others? Give examples.

Day 2:
Read Romans 14
and answer the following questions:
- Who was the weaker brother noted here? Explain how you arrived at this answer.
- How can the love of God direct you to the correct attitude toward others with different opinions?

Day 3:

Read Romans 15

and answer the following questions:

- How does Christ's example lead us to correct love for one another?
- How does love assist you to have empathy for those you have never met? Consider Paul's pleading in verses 30–33.

Day 4:

Read Romans 16

and answer the following questions:

- Why was Paul's list of people whom he loved so long? Explain.
- How long a list do you have of people you love? And how long a list of people do you have whom you do not love?

Day 5:

Read Exodus 20

and answer the following questions:

- Why did God choose ten commandments and not twenty? Prove your answer.
- Which commandments do you struggle to keep? Be honest. This is for your growth.

I think Mark Twain said that a lie runs around the world while truth is putting on her shoes.

* * * * * * * *

WEEK TWENTY

Watch Out
2 John 1:7–13

- - - - - - - -

I have an uncle on my dad's side of the family who has a habit of always saying one phrase when something either is dangerous or startles him. He says with great emotion, "Look out!" Sadly, he has said it so much that most people who know him only laugh when he says it. However there have been extremely dangerous moments when he has sounded a warning by saying, "Look out!" and had to go to the next level of actually pushing someone out of the way of danger.

You and I are in week 20 of our devotions together. We began by studying 1 John, which clearly taught us about who Jesus was and is. In chapter 2 John repeatedly reminded us to beware of false teachers. I can hear him crying, "Look out!"

Now we are in 2 John, and once again John takes his wick in hand and writes to us about false teachers in our present text. Here he uses a phrase similar to what my uncle would use: *Watch out* (NLT). Jesus gives the same warning in Mark 13:9, but with an even stronger phrase: *Be on your guard.*

The issue on John's heart is one of great importance. It involves the souls of people who have not been saved, and it involves the rewards of those who have been saved. The apostle John loved this church, and he wanted it to be successful to its fullest potential. He knew that if the church allowed these false teachers to infiltrate their house churches, the consequences would be grave.

Notice how John describes these false teachers in verse 7. They make up a large group of people known as deceivers. These apostate teachers cause people to make mistakes in their theology and in their practices of life. John warned us in 1 John 2:26, "[They] are trying to deceive you." These apostles deny Jesus' coming in the flesh, and in doing so they deny His deity as well. Warren Wierbse commented on this: "They give their converts a substitute Christ" (*The Bible Exposition Commentary,* vol. 1, 274).

John's words of warning in verse 8 are in the strongest of terms. He is pleading with this lady to make sure she and other leaders in the church keep the deceivers out of their church, their homes, and their hearts. As I read those words, I understand that John is warning the church to be prepared—because they are coming. I want you to know this. This is not something that was happening only in the first century. It happens all the time in the church today. Yes, we have moved away from house churches and have constructed church buildings. But into our church buildings come those who teach falsely. I remember several years ago a person coming to our church proclaiming the King James Version of the Bible as God's only authorized version. For a while we attempted to work with this person, but each day I had the uneasy conviction from God, "Watch out." Within a year we had to ask this person to leave. It became clear that this man believed many false doctrines.

The Bible is clear:

- Godly leaders watch out for our souls (Hebrews 13:17).
- We must test all our teachers (1 Timothy 4:16).
- Satan tempts all leaders to compromise (Galatians 6:1).
- People are always trying to cause division (Romans 16:17).

John knows that if false teachers are allowed and embraced, the church will lose what it has gained. In this moment we need to ask ourselves, "What has the church gained?" The church has gained the truth of who God is, and it has gained influence in the community. Finally, the church has gained reward in heaven for its labor of love.

With the embracing of false teaching, all of this will go down the drain. The warning here is so real. How many are the New Testament churches that have lost their witness and have lost their way because of leaders who have chosen to walk away from the truth?

It is clear in verse 9 that such leaders will push forward in their mistakes. They embrace a life of preaching a cover-up message of liberty. They call evil good and good evil. Such leaders are not truly Christ-followers. They do not have God and they certainly cannot have God.

The apostle Paul warned the church in Corinth of this same reality: "I am afraid that, as the serpent deceived Eve by his craftiness, your minds will be led astray from the simplicity and purity of devotion to Christ" (2 Corinthians 11:3).

Now, for some who read this, great fear comes because you wonder if you could be led away from Christ. It is clear from verse 9 that if you stay with the truth of God's Word, you will remain in Him. Many who do not know the truth are led away, and many who forget the truth walk away from what is right. But it does not have to be so among us.

We need to heed John's warning: "Watch out."

In verses 10–11 we find practical ways to ensure that we watch out:

1. Refuse to allow false teachers into your church, your home, and your heart.
2. Refuse to endorse someone's false views by not participating in their sinful acts.
3. Resolve to walk with pastors and churches that both teach and model the Word of God.

These three practical applications sometimes come under the strong scrutiny of people who say that you're being legalistic. Such critics say you can never reach lost people this way. My brothers and sisters, we are not talking about isolating ourselves from lost people. We open our homes to lost people all the time seeking to build bridges to the gospel with them. The issue here is apostate teachers and followers who are proclaiming untruth. To such moments John cries, "Watch out!"

This week's daily readings will help us to think even more deeply on this subject:

Day 1:
Read Galatians 1
and answer the following questions:

- Why did certain members of this church turn away so quickly from the gospel?
- What did God have to reveal to Paul before he would embrace Christianity?

Day 2:

Read Galatians 2

and answer the following questions:

- Why does religion that promises liberty really end up producing slavery? Hint: verse 4 will help in your answer.
- Explain what Paul means in verses 15–17.

Day 3:

Read Galatians 3–4

and answer the following questions:

- What role does the Holy Spirit play in our salvation?
- What is the blessing of Abraham?

Day 4:

Read Galatians 5

and answer the following questions:

- How does one stand firm in the freedom of Christ?
- What does the fruit of the Spirit look like in a 21st-century believer?

Day 5:

Read Galatians 6

and answer the following questions:

- How much sin do we have to commit in order for us to lose our salvation?

- When should we give up on trying to reach lost people?

* * * * * * * *

WEEK TWENTY-ONE

Helping Others
3 John 1:1–8

Their names may never appear on the pages of history, but in my mind these names are very important: Phil and Linda Bentley. They are very important because they gave themselves to helping others. When Sherry and I were just beginning in ministry, they reached out to us to become ministry partners with us. They provided a place for us to live our first year and cared for us for our first five years in ministry. Over the years there have been many other names added to our list of those who have helped others.

Question: Would your name make anyone's list of those who helped others?

As John the elder writes his third letter, he addresses it to a man simply known as Gaius. All we know about Gaius is that he is a "well-beloved" (KJV) friend of John.

Keep in mind, John is pastoring in Ephesus and apparently is the overseer for churches in the region. Gaius was a leader in the church in his area. John writes to him knowing there is a great problem in the church. We will speak to the problem next week.

But this week we focus on Gaius, who was a well-beloved believer who walked in truth. This truth led him to be an example in helping others. This man so impacted John that John offers a personal prayer for him. It is a prayer I have offered many times for people who help others. Look closely at it:

- John desires for the activities of Gaius's life to be successful.

Of course, we know some activities of men that we hope are not successful. For such activity we offer no prayer. John wishes the Father to bless this man in his activity. We know, according to 1 John 5:13–14, that if we are actively doing the will of God we will have the requests we ask.

- John desires for God to bless Gaius's health and spirit.

A person who helps others often wears out his or her body trying to help others. Such people need the supernatural power of God's strength. Paul understood this as he indicates in 2 Corinthians 12:9–10. Gaius was walking in the truth. Others had shared their experiences of Gaius being helpful to them.

As I worked through this text I began to pray for myself: "Dear Father, I want to be one who is helpful to others. I want my family to be helpful to others."

We see John's heart being filled with joy because of the brothers and sisters walking in truth. I identify with John because I pastor a church that helps others in amazing ways. I shepherd people who live lives of godliness. God is giving them everything they need to walk the walk (2 Peter 1:3–4). I pray that this devotion spurs you to join their number.

As John moves into the body of his letter, he gives us an example of Gaius helping others. Notice verses 5 and 6. This man was opening his home to the traveling evangelists coming through his area. The work of the evangelist was so important in John's day (Ephesians 4:11–12) as it is in our day. These evangelists relied on the love and care of God's people to be able to do what they did. Others would shy away from strangers, but this brother reached out because these were God's servants. These men testified of Gaius's care for them.

Question: Do people testify of our care of others?

Gaius was sending these evangelists out to other towns knowing he had supplied their needs. The apostle Paul commended the church at Philippi (Philippians 4:14–19) for helping him in this same way. In our minds we must ask this question: "How can people do this?" The answer is simple: Gaius treated others in the same way he would treat Jesus.

Paul challenges the church in Ephesus (5:2) to "walk in love, just as Christ also loved you and gave Himself up for us" (NASB). Can you and I read these verses in 3 John and claim to be in the same category as Gaius?

The evangelists could affirm they were loved, because Gaius loved the Lord. When it comes to helping others, the following should govern our actions:

1. We need to know what a worthy manner looks like. For me, it is sacrificing what is valuable to God because I love Him (2 Corinthians 9:6–7).

2. We need to consider the return:
   a. We are rewarded here (Matthew 7:12; 19:29–30).
   b. We are rewarded in heaven (Matthew 10:42; Luke 6:31–36; Matthew 6:19–24).

3. We need to consider how we are entering into partnership with those we give help.

Gaius did not just blindly give to everyone. He gave to those who needed help and those who would use it for the correct purpose. There are many ways to enter into such partnership. We partner financially, prayerfully, and in personal teamwork for the sake of the gospel.

John challenges the entire church to support others by helping them.

As I came to this point in my studies, God invaded my thinking. He led me to write down names of the helpers in my life. As I did, tears flowed because a few of those are now in heaven. But for those who are still alive, I offered prayer and sent letters thanking those saints of God for being helpers in my life. I also got onto my knees and sought God's wisdom in how to be a better helper to others for the sake of the gospel.

This week's readings will challenge us to take risks for the sake of others:

Day 1:
Read Esther 1–2
and answer the following questions:
- Would there have been anyone you would have wanted to help in the first chapter of Esther? Give reasons why or why not.
- How could Esther becoming queen be of help to others? Wasn't she being selfish in wanting to be queen? Give reasons.

Day 2:

Read Esther 3–4

and answer the following questions:

- Why would Haman want to kill God's people?
- Why did Mordecai believe Esther had been brought to the kingdom for such a time as this?

Day 3:

Read Esther 5–6

and answer the following questions:

- How could simple things such as hosting a banquet make a difference in people's lives?
- How did Mordecai's kindness pay off in chapter 5?

Day 4:

Read Esther 7–8

and answer the following questions:

- How did Esther put her life on the line for her own people? How far would you go to help the people called your fellow men?
- What was Esther's plan to rescue her people, and what is your plan to rescue your fellow men?

Day 5:

Read Esther 9–10

and answer the following questions:

- How can going to war sometimes help others, or does it ever help others? Defend your answer.
- How will God reward you as one who helps others?

* * * * * * * *

WEEK TWENTY-TWO

The Story of a Dictator
3 John 1:9–13

One of my favorite pictures is that of an African elephant that is on my laptop screen saver. Every time I see it I am reminded to pray for the people of Malawi. When I think about the elephant, I sometimes think about the bad rap elephants get when it comes to the following idiom: "There's an elephant in the room." This idiom suggests that there is a problem in the room that no one wants to discuss.

I want you to know this fact: if there is an elephant in the room with me, I am going to discuss it as I leave the room.

The truth is, there is an elephant in the room in 3 John. John writes to commend Gaius for being a great helper in the gospel. He and the church have a desire to bless the evangelists who are blessing them. But not everyone in

Gaius' church feels this way. There is a guy who is doing his best to keep the church from being hospitable.

John writes, *I have written something to the church.* Apparently this person had refused to allow anyone else to read this something. His name was Diotrephes. His elephant-like behavior can be compared to that of a dictator.

Question: Are there any dictators in your church? Now I know this may be an elephant-like discussion, but it is one we need to have. I have met people who have had the following view: "Oh, they're just like that, and we just overlook them." Take a few moments with me and imagine what you are trying to overlook:

1. **You are trying to overlook a person who is putting *himself or herself first.***

Diotrephes, according to the KJV, "loveth to have the preeminence" in the church. Think through this. Here was a man who wanted to have the first position in the church. He wanted to be honored over the Lord. Colossians 1:18 stresses this fact: "He is the head of the body, the church. He is the beginning, the firstborn from the dead, that in everything he might be preeminent." The glory belongs to God alone. This is His church (Ephesians 1:22–23).

However, Diotrephes had the constant attitude of being the one in charge. Now let the elephant out: we all struggle with this in our flesh. In Matthew 18 the apprentices also struggled with it. But those who have the love of God, the truth of God, and are serving God will overcome for the glory of God.

Not Diotrephes—he was going to have the glory. John the elder makes it clear (v. 10) that if he comes he will deal with this dictator.

2. You are trying to overlook a person who is *sabotaging* the church.

Diotrephes was standing strongly against anyone who wanted to help others for the glory of God. He was speaking falsely against John and the elders of the church. The Holman Christian Standard Bible translates that part of verse 10 as "[He is] slandering us with malicious words."

Does this go on in your church? I am so thankful that I lead a church that helps others and seeks to build up others. But even in our church there are those few who, if left to their own desires, would sabotage our church. Be assured that the Lord stands up against such people (Leviticus 19:16). In 3 John the church is being encouraged to stand up against this guy.

3. You are trying to overlook a person who is *keeping* you from freely and fully serving the Lord.

Diotrephes refused to be hospitable, and he would not tell anyone in the church to be hospitable. He was truly a dictator in the church. He was even going to the extent of running people away who tried to make difference with others. It's the elephant in the room, but it is true: this was all about Diotrephes. This man wanted everything for himself.

In this moment I want to pause and reflect. This man's dictatorship has raised many people's minds and hearts to previous memories or present actions now. I have known such people who have run off godly church members who wanted to serve but did not know how to overcome Diotrephes.

The elephant in the room is not the question of whether we need to acknowledge such people. The elephant in the room is how to we handle such people. We find our answer in verse 11:

Do not imitate evil but imitate good.

John shows us the way. There are no fewer than four steps we need to take to dethrone all earthly dictators in the church:

- Stay away from such people. "Follow not" (v. 11, KJV) such people. Never allow them to have influence in your life (Psalm 34:11–18).

- Stop being such a person. We must check our own hearts (Psalm 139:23–24). God has called us to be cleansed from the old man (Isaiah 1:16–18).
- Start being a sanctified person. God wants us to live a life of putting God first and others second. We are to put on the mind of Christ (Philippians 2:1–5).
- Stand against dictators in love. Allow God to use you to be His instrument of a different way of living (1 Timothy 6:4).

This week's readings will charge us to a better way to live:

Day 1:

Read Titus 1

and answer the following questions:

- If you were Titus, how would you attempt to set things in order in your church? Be careful not to give names in your answer.
- What does it mean to rebuke someone sharply?

Day 2:

Read Titus 2

and answer the following questions:

- How important is it to have mentors mentoring younger members in the church?
- What are the biblical qualifications of a mentor?

Day 3:

Read Titus 3

and answer the following questions:

- How hard is it to carry out verses 1–2? Explain.
- What does it mean to have nothing to do with someone, according to verse 10?

Day 4:

Read Philemon 1

and answer the following questions:

- How did Paul approach trying to reconcile the breach between the brothers in Philemon?
- To what lengths was Paul willing to go to see this situation reconciled? To what lengths are you willing to go to overcome dictators in the church?

Day 5:

Read Jude 1

and answer the following questions:

- Why did Jude feel he had to contend for the common faith?
- How can dictators destroy the common faith?

CONCLUSION

I know you often hear this and sometimes wonder if it is true. But I promise you that it is true. This study of 1, 2, and 3 John has radically changed my life. I have read through these letters many times over the last twenty-six years. And on two occasions I attempted to preach through these books. Both times I was called away to other churches as I prepared to teach them.

So naturally I was nervous about beginning the study. Also, while in seminary I had to write a commentary on 3 John as my final in a class titled "Inductive Bible Study." I found the commentary and made an A on the writing only because of the grace of God. I really had no clue as to what I was writing—a large portion of the material consisted of quotes cited from other sources.

Now all these years later, I write these last lines in our study with tears in my eyes. How can anyone truly study these letters without becoming a believer who loves more, knows more about Jesus, and serves others better because of the love of Jesus being poured out in his or her life?

Before this study I thought I knew what these letters were about, but now I realize I am just beginning to understand the depths and heights of God's love for me. I am just beginning to understand who God is and what knowing Him and loving Him does in altering my life.

As you come to the end of this book, may 1 John always be your reminder of the humanity of Jesus and His love for us. May you always love others. Never again skip over 2 John. Truth must be guarded, and truth must be championed by the people who love God and for the sake of those who do not love God. Always linger in 3 John to be reminded of the importance of being hospitable to all people as well as avoiding dictatorship in the church.

Thank you so much for walking with me these many weeks. I leave you with the words of John from 1 John 3:16:

By this we know love, that he laid down his life for us, and we ought to lay down our lives for the brothers.

* * * * * * * *

WORKS CITED

Allan, David. *1–3 John, Preaching the Word.* Wheaton, Ill.: Crossway Publishing, 2013.

Bennett, Roy. A Summary of the Westminister Confession of Faith. christchurchventura.org.

Grudem, Wayne. *Systematic Theology.* Grand Rapids: Zondervan, 2000.

Jeremiah, David. *I Never Thought I'd See the Day!* New York: Faith Words, 2014.

MacArthur, John. *MacArthur New Testament Commentary, 1–3 John.* Chicago: Moody Publishers, 2007.

Spurgeon, C. H. *Morning and Evening Prayer.* New Kensington, Pa.: Whitaker House, 1997.

Wiersbe, Warren. *The Bible Exposition Commentary. Vol. 1.* Colorado Springs: Chariot Victor Publishing, 2000.

www.ingramcontent.com/pod-product-compliance
Lightning Source LLC
La Vergne TN
LVHW011332080426
835513LV00006B/299